# WINE IN
# THE ANCIENT
# WORLD

CHARLES SELTMAN

Litt.D., formerly Fellow of Queens' College
and Lecturer in Classical Archaeology
in the University of Cambridge

Routledge & Kegan Paul Ltd
LONDON

*First published 1957*
© *by Routledge & Kegan Paul Limited*
*Broadway House, 68-74 Carter Lane*
*London, E.C.4*

*Made and printed in Great Britain*
*by William Clowes and Sons, Limited*
*London and Beccles*

To

DIONYSOS AND ARIADNE

# PREFACE

ONE hundred and thirty-four years ago an elegant volume was produced having been written by a certain Mr Henderson living in "Curzon Street, London" entitled *The History of Ancient and Modern Wines*. It was published by Baldwin, Cradock and Joy in Paternoster Row in the year of grace eighteen hundred and twenty-four. Part I of this work, which ran to one hundred and twenty-eight pages, was a history of ancient wines. Since that date—as far as I am aware—no book has appeared in the English language dealing with our subject; though, of course, articles have occurred in the various Dictionaries. When Mr Henderson wrote his learned work, the science of archaeology was as yet unborn. Minoans were unheard of; the Mycenaean phase of Hellenic life unimagined; Athenian vases were called Tuscan urns and ancient coins were dubbed medals. Yet as will appear in the following pages, archaeology has been able to contribute far more to our knowledge about wine and the gods of wine in the ancient world than ever could have been imagined at the beginning of the last century.

The central theme of Chapter 11, which I have entitled "Roman Banquet", is one of the world's supreme farces. Everyone who is caught by the fascination of the *Satyricon* of Gaius Petronius tries to make his own translation. Mine is only partly original because I have been helped and my task has been lightened by a study of Michael Heseltine's version (in the Loeb Classical Library) of the passages describing the banquet of Trimalchio. I have deliberately made my brief excerpts much more colloquial.

When an author completes a book he is always aware of the debt of gratitude that he owes to other people. I should like to mention in particular Mr Ronald Crosland, Mr Henry St J. Hart, Mr John Leatham, Dr N. M. Penzer and Dr R. B. Whitehead.

Cambridge 1957                                                  C. S.

# ACKNOWLEDGMENTS

THE author's thanks are due to the following for permitting quotations: George G. Harrap & Co. Ltd (H. B. Cotterill's *Odyssey*); Mr F. L. Lucas and J. M. Dent & Co. (three poems in *Greek Poetry for Everyman*); Mr D. W. Lucas and the Cambridge Greek Play Committee (*Euripides' Bacchae*); Dr E. V. Rieu and Penguin Books Ltd (*Odyssey and Iliad*); The Clarendon Press, Oxford (three poems in *The Oxford Book of Greek Verse in Translation*); John Lehmann Ltd (Christopher Kininmonth, *The Children of Thetis*); The Cambridge University Press (seven blocks from A. B. Cook's *Zeus*); and the Editors of *History Today* for allowing the author to quote from his own articles.

# CONTENTS

|    | PREFACE | vii |
|----|---------|-----|
| 1  | SYMPOSIUM: A PARTY IN ATHENS | 1 |
| 2  | ORIGINS OF WINE | 14 |
| 3  | WINE IN THE HEROIC AGE | 32 |
| 4  | THE THIRTEENTH GOD | 49 |
| 5  | VINTAGE | 67 |
| 6  | BOTTLES, BEAKERS AND CUPS | 82 |
| 7  | WINE, WOMEN . . . | 95 |
| 8  | . . . AND SONG | 110 |
| 9  | THE TRADE | 129 |
| 10 | DE BACCHANALIBUS | 144 |
| 11 | ROMAN BANQUET | 156 |
| 12 | CONTINUITY | 173 |
|    | BIBLIOGRAPHY | 183 |
|    | INDEX | 185 |

# LIST OF FIGURES

*Figure*                                                            *Page*

1 Drawing after a red figure vase painting by the
  Marlay painter, *c.* 430 B.C. Naked dancing girl and
  boy with lyre. In Leningrad (*Compte Rendu,* 1864,
  183)                                                                 12

2 The peasant God from Ivriz (A. B. Cook, *Zeus,*
  Vol. I, Fig. 453)                                                    22

3 Two silver coins of Tarsus minted by the Satrap
  Datames (378 to 374 B.C.) representing the local Wine
  God (A. B. Cook, *Zeus,* Vol. I, Figs. 454, 455)                     23

4 Bronze statuette of Priapos found at Lampsacus,
  height 3·1 inches when complete, fourth century
  B.C. (by courtesy of the owner)                                      29

5 Limestone drum, 0·84 metres height from Les
  Fontaines now at Brussels representing naked
  Bacchant. (A. B. Cook, *Zeus,* Vol. II, Fig. 32)                     64

6 Engraved gem in Florence depicting Bacchant milking her own breast into a vase. (A. B. Cook, *Zeus,*
  Vol. II, Fig. 241)                                                   65

7 Attic black-figure vase painting, *c.* 550–540 B.C.
  Peasants and boys collecting grapes from a climbing
  vine. In the Louvre                                                  69

7a Attic black-figure vase painting by the Amasis
  painter, *c.* 550 B.C. The whole process of vintage
  with Satyrs impersonating peasants. In Würtzburg
  (p. 87)                                                              70

8 Stemmed Kylix                                                        84

9 Kylix                                                                84

10 Krater (Column-krater)                                             85

11 Volute-krater                                                      85

# LIST OF FIGURES

12 Krater (Bell-krater)                                                    85
13 Kalyx-krater                                                            85
14 Hydria                                                                  86
15 Amphora                                                                 89
16 Amphora                                                                 89
17 Nolan Amphora                                                           89
18 Kantharos                                                               90
19 Kotyle                                                                  90
20 Dionysos holding Kantharos and grapes seated on
   winged car preceded by Seilenos carrying vases
   (A. B. Cook, *Zeus*, Vol. I, Fig. 158b)                               103
21 Map of the Aegean showing wine-growing states                         134
22 Coin list of wine states in the Aegean Regions                        135
23 Map of South Italy and Sicily showing certain wine-
   growing states                                                        139
24 Coin list of wine states in Western Greek regions                     140

# LIST OF PLATES

*Plate*            *Between pp. 80 and 81*

I    Attic red figure vase painting inside a Kylix painted by Epiktetos, *c.* 500 B.C. Boy with flutes and dancing girl with castanets. In the British Museum. (*F.R.*, Pl. 73)

II    Attic red figure vase painting inside a Kylix painted by the Gales painter, *c.* 500 B.C. Youth embracing flute-girl. In Yale (Baur, *Yale Catalogue*, 1922, Pl. 15)

III    Attic red figure vase painting outside a Kylix painted by the Foundry painter, *c.* 480 B.C. Naked flute-girl and revellers. In Corpus Christi College, Cambridge. (*J.H.S.*, 41, Pl. 16)

IV    Attic red figure vase painting inside a Kylix painted by the Brygos painter, *c.* 470 B.C. Youth and dancing girl named Pilipos and Kalisto. In the British Museum (*Catal. Murray*, No. 47)

V    Attic red figure vase painting on a hydria painted by Polygnotos, *c.* 440 B.C. Girls dancing and tumbling. In Naples. (*F.R.*, Vol. III, pp. 320–1)

VI    Attic red figure volute-Krater painted by the Pronomos painter, *c.* 410 B.C. Part of a stage scene showing young Dionysos and Ariadne embracing. In Naples (*F.R.*, 143–5)

VII    "The Cup of Nestor." Gold, with double handles and two doves perched by the rim, *c.* 1250, B.C. From Mycenae, in Athens

VIII    (*a* and *b*) Part of the Hubbard Amphora, *c.* 900 B.C. A lady drinking wine from a syphon; on the left a Bull's Head Rhyton. In the Archaeological Museum, at Nicosia, Cyprus. (*B.S.A.*, 37, Pl. 8) (by courtesy of Mr Dikaios)

xv

*Plate*

IX    Minoan Steatite Bull's Head Rhyton for pouring wine, *c.* 1450 B.C. Height 7·1 inches (the horns are modern). (By courtesy of the owner)

X    Shallow silver wine cup, diam. 8·8 inches, about 250 B.C. From Tarentum. Inside in high relief Dionysos and Ariadne kissing; a thyrsos between them. (Compare Pl. VI.) Seltman, *Approach to Greek Art*, Pl. 90

XI    Attic red figure vase from Camirus (early fourth century B.C.) with scene from a comedy (A. B. Cook, *Zeus*, Vol. I, Pl. XXXVI)

XII    Attic red figure vase painting on the outside of a Kylix painted by Makron, *c.* 490 B.C. Six Athenian Thyiads or Maenads. Another six are on the other side. (In Berlin)

XIII    Top of a bronze Kottabos-stand decorated with a sphinx seated upon an Ionian capital. Perhaps Ionian work about 450–400 B.C. By courtesy of the owners, Messrs Spink & Son

XIV    Coins of various wine-producing states.

(1) Peparethos, silver, *c.* 500 B.C. Bunch of grapes and Eros

(2) Mende, silver, *c.* 430 B.C. Dionysos on ass and small vine in a square

(3) Trapezus, silver, *c.* 410 B.C. Male head, and table loaded with grapes

(4) Rhodes, gold, *c.* 400 B.C. Head of Helios and rose beside which bunch of grapes

(5) Chios, copper, *c.* 200 B.C. Sphinx and pointed wine amphora

(6) Naxos in Sicily, silver, *c.* 460 B.C. Head of Dionysos and squatting Seilenos with wine cup

XV    Greek pottery wine amphora from Skiathos (1956) found in the sea, off Cape Artemision. Height 17 inches. (By courtesy of the owner)

XVI    The Corycian plain, 4000 feet above sea-level, looking east to the summit of Parnassus. Photograph by the author taken in 1925

*Chapter One*

❖❖❖❖❖❖❖❖❖❖❖❖❖❖❖❖❖❖❖❖❖❖❖❖❖❖❖❖❖❖❖❖❖❖❖❖❖❖❖❖❖❖❖

# SYMPOSIUM:
# A PARTY IN ATHENS

❖❖❖❖❖❖❖❖❖❖❖❖❖❖❖❖❖❖❖❖❖❖❖❖❖❖❖❖❖❖❖❖❖❖❖❖❖❖❖❖❖❖❖

DIONYSOS as god of wine gives either fear or consolation; and, although other substances besides wine are his concern, it is by wine that there comes to mankind either brutishness or brilliance. Befuddled the brain goes to pieces; enlivened the mind expands ripe with genial and civilised reflections; for the god can give either the desolation of the drunkard's anguished brow, or the delight and sparkle of quickened life. Such joy, under the gentler influence of Dionysos, must often have existed in congenial company in ancient Athens, when at some well-moderated symposium, or supper-party, Attic intellects sparkled under the beneficent influence of wine. Moderation normally ruled in Athenian Society of the fifth century B.C. and therefore wine proved to be the finest tonic in the lives of civilised men. A proper approach to the customs of those days may best be made by the description of supper-parties in Athens such as have been recorded by two eminent disciples of Socrates.

Plato and Xenophon wrote, each of them, a sketch called the *Symposium*, and in both these brilliant stories Socrates played the main rôle. But the two descriptions of these events in fifth-century Athens are very different in tone because they describe two very different parties. Seriousness with profundity—though never pedantry—was the keynote of Plato's *Symposium* written about 385 B.C. Gaiety and inconsequence pervaded Xenophon's

I

party, mainly because there was what is now called a "floor-show", very much in our twentieth-century style. The interruptions caused by such a performance do not make for fluent or closely argued philosophic disquisitions, since attention wanders to the performers. Plato's dialogue has always been well known among scholars and has achieved a wider appeal since a new and brilliant translation recently appeared.[1] The other dialogue, or sketch, is much less familiar, because it has been neglected, perhaps on account of its flippancy and comparative lack of elevating sentiments. The fact that the Platonic *Symposium* is written in praise of homosexual love fails to repel some readers, who might well regard Xenophon's *Symposium* with disfavour because of the healthy heterosexual end to the story. In the former conversation has not been going for long before Socrates is made to suggest that they send away the little flute-girl and concentrate on solemn things. In the latter the little flute-girl receives all encouragement, as do her two accomplished young companions, the "Stars" of the floor-show. Further comment on Xenophon's *Symposium* is clearly desirable.[2]

It was all delightfully casual, even as it might be now in a wealthy Athenian household which did not lack for good service. Kallias, in the summer of 421 B.C., was giving a party in his fine house in Piraeus as the Greater Panathenaic Games had just come to an end. A boy, Autolykos son of Lykaon, remarkable for his physical beauty, had been featuring in an important event: the Pankration. This was a severe athletic contest involving a combination of boxing and wrestling, and required on the part of the competitors particular excellence of physique and training. There were, of course, separate events; some for men, some for youths, some for boys. The victory of Autolykos was the excuse for giving the party. As Kallias and his friends were making their way from the Athenian Stadium to Piraeus they fell

---

[1] *Plato, The Symposium*, transl. W. Hamilton (Penguin Classics, L 24), 1951.
[2] There is an excellent translation by O. J. Todd, *Xenophon*, in the Loeb Classical Library (1922).

in with a group including Socrates and several of his friends and disciples. "This is a fortunate meeting," said Kallias, "for I am about to give a dinner in honour of Autolykos and his father; and I think that my entertainment would acquire more brilliance if my dining-room were graced by the presence of men like you, whose hearts have undergone philosophy's purification than it would be with generals, or cavalry officers, or politicians." At first Socrates and his companions expressed polite thanks for the invitation but would not promise to accept; but when it became evident that Kallias was taking their refusal very much to heart they agreed to follow him. And so some of his guests having taken their exercise, a shower and a rub down, others a bath, the company assembled. Autolykos took his seat by his father's side; and the men, as was the custom, reclined.

Imagination pictures a large room in the house of Kallias where the entertainment took place. For each of the distinguished guests there was placed a couch with a mattress and several cushions, and these couches would be arranged in a wide semi-circle, or horsehoe with an open space, as though it might be a dance-floor, between. In front of each couch there was placed a small elegant "occasional table" on which the food was served in individual dishes and which left room for a wine-cup and a bowl of fruit. In the summer weather of Greece people require much smaller quantities of food than are consumed in our northern latitudes. Bread and a little meat, or fish perhaps, fresh vegetables and fruit; if any drink was taken with these comestibles it was certainly diluted with water. Only when all the guests had finished eating did the serious business of the Symposium—a word which means "drinking together"—begin. The host, or president of the party, would decide on the mixture of wine and water: two parts wine and one part water; or, more often, half and half. Conversation, serious or flippant, entertainment and gaiety, now filled the long evening and night, often into the early morning hours.

The boy Autolykos with his modesty and good manners, wreathed in the glamour of his victory in the Games, was the centre of attraction and in a strange way of embarrassment; and,

3

as the tables were placed and the food served by the attendants, the party seemed at first to hang fire. The company was dining in silence when there was a knock at the door and the porter announced that Philip, a professional Funny Man, asked to be admitted, giving the message that with regard to food he had come prepared to dine on some other persons' provisions, and that his manservant was in great distress with the load which he carried of—nothing, and with having an empty stomach. When Kallias heard this he said, "Well, gentlemen, we cannot really begrudge him the shelter of our roof; so let him come in." Philip appeared at the door and greeted the company with the words, "You all know I'm a professional Funny Man and at the moment I think it is a better joke to come to your dinner uninvited than by invitation." "All right," said Kallias, "take a couch; and you will notice that your fellow guests although well fed on seriousness are rather lacking in laughter."

As the dinner went on Philip attempted a wise-crack which fell flat. Annoyed at this, he tried another one a little later, got no laughter, and so lay down full length on his couch covering his head with a cloak. The host asked if he was seized with pain and Philip groaning replied, "Yes, by Zeus, a bad one, Kallias, because laughter seems to have perished from the world and so my job is ruined. Why, in the past one got invitations to dine in order to make people laugh; but who is going to invite me now? Seriousness? Impossible from me!" And when he appeared to be weeping one of the guests burst into a guffaw at his moaning noises. This had the right effect on Philip who uncovered his head and started once more to eat heartily.

Dinner was over; the attendants removed the tables with the remnants of the food; a libation of wine was poured to the appropriate gods and a hymn was sung, as it might be "Grace after meat". Perhaps it was at this point that a decision was made as to the precise mixture of wine and water which was to be used for the rest of the evening. Meanwhile Kallias' butler, who had already arranged for the *divertissement*, announced that the performers were ready, and there entered a man from Syracuse pre-

4

pared to give them an evening's entertainment. He had with him a fine flute-girl, and a dancing-girl—one of those who were clever at acrobatic tricks—and a very good-looking boy who was an expert at playing the lyre and at dancing. This Syracusan made a handsome income by organising performances of the kind that was to follow. First they played for the company, the flute-girl on her double-flutes and the boy on the lyre and all agreed that they were good entertainers. Socrates himself remarked: "By Zeus, Kallias, you are giving us a good feast; not only have you set before us a meal that is above criticism, but here you are offering us delectable sights and sounds." Gratified, Kallias replied, "Shall we go further and shall I order some perfume so that we may dine in the midst of pleasant odours too?" "No, no," said Socrates, "for, just as one kind of dress looks well on a woman and another kind on a man, so the odours appropriate to men and to women are different. No man, surely, ever uses perfume for a man's sake.3 And as for women, particularly if they happen to be young brides, like the wives of your two guests here, Nikeratos and Kritoboulos, how can they want any additional perfumes? For that is what they are redolent of themselves."

Perfume, it seemed, was about to become a topic for philosophic discussion when Socrates, his eye on the door, said, "Let us reserve this for some other time and concentrate now on the matter at hand; for I see that the dancing-girl here is standing all ready and that someone is bringing her some hoops."

The floor-show had started, for the other girl gave her a tune on the flutes and the boy beside her gradually handed her the little hoops until he had passed her as many as twelve which she took and, as she danced—naked like her companions—kept throwing them spinning into the air and catching them in perfect rhythm. Socrates, looking on, began to comment, " Gentlemen," he said, " what this girl is doing is surely but one of many proofs

3 If, as is probable, Xenophon was quoting an actual remark made by Socrates then these words—indeed the whole short speech—are evidence for the normal heterosexual inclinations of Socrates.

that woman's nature is really not at all inferior to man's"; and he advised those who had wives to teach them whatever they wished for they would learn anything as easily as a man. One of the guests asked Socrates why he didn't practise what he was preaching by exerting his influence on Xanthippe—about the most difficult wife any man could have to live with! "Men who want to become expert horsemen," replied Socrates, "don't ride gentle horses but those which are full of mettle, thinking that if they can manage the latter they can handle any horse. My intention was similar; for it is mankind in general that I wish to deal with and to understand and so I married Xanthippe, knowing that if I could put up with her I should have no difficulty with the rest of humankind."

Reflection causes one to doubt whether Socrates would ever have made a successful Petruchio because Xanthippe [4] must have been a more long-suffering woman than Katherina.

Attention was now turned to the floor-show, for the servants brought in a great metal circle set all around with upright swords and over these the naked dancing-girl turned somersaults into the circle and out again, an act which rather dismayed the spectators who were afraid that she might suffer an accident. She, however, went through the performance gaily and safely. Socrates, of course, must have his comment, remarking that anyone who saw this feat would never again deny that courage was something which could be taught when one saw that gentle girl leaping so bravely among the swords.

"Ah!" said Antisthenes, one of the guests, "this Syracusan ought to exhibit his dancing-girl to the whole city of Athens and announce that if they will pay him well he will give all Athenians courage to face the point of a sword." "Good!" Philip remarked, "I'd like to see the politician Peisander learning to turn somersaults among knives. As things are now his panic when he looks at spears stops him even from enlisting."

And now the boy performed a dance causing Socrates to

4 See an intriguing fantasy by Wilfranc Hubbard, in *Tanagra Figures* (1927), Chapter II, "An Apology for Xanthippe".

6

remark that the lad, handsome as he was, appeared even more so when his body was in graceful well-balanced movements. These words led to a discussion among the diners concerning the virtue of dancing as a healthful exercise. Raillery of Socrates himself entered into this discussion, since a middle-aged man of his figure would appear clownish hopping around on the floor. Philip, the Funny Man, felt moved to make a contribution to all this and asked the flute-girl to play a measure for him. He then proceeded to mimic in detail the dancing, first of the boy and then of the girl, making a burlesque of the boy's movements by letting his limbs assume grotesque attitudes; and, while the girl had bent backward until she resembled a hoop, he copied this by bending forward. Then, so as to have a real fling, he told the flute-girl to hit up the time faster and danced off tossing legs, arms and head all at the same time, until he collapsed in exhaustion on his couch. "Good exercise, gentlemen," he panted, "and it's given me a good thirst. Boy, fill me a big goblet!" "A round for all of us," cried Kallias, "we're all thirsty with laughing at you."

It appeared that Socrates must once again become sententious; for indeed, the company expected this of him. "Gentlemen, so far as drinking is concerned you have my approval, wine moistens the soul and lulls our griefs to sleep while it also awakens kindly feelings. Yet I suspect that men's bodies react like those of growing plants. When a god gives plants too much water to drink they can't stand up straight and the winds flatten them; but when they drink exactly what they require they grow straight and tall and bear abundant fruit. And so it is with us. We pour ourselves great draughts and before long our bodies and our minds reel and we talk nonsense; but if the servants constantly keep filling small cups we are brought by the gentle persuasion of the wine to a gayer mood."

Applause followed.

The boy now came forward, tuned his lyre to the girl's double-flutes, and played and sang to the delight of all; and one of the guests remarked that what Socrates had said about the wine had its complement in this blending of the young people's beauty with the notes of the music which lulled one's grief to sleep and awakened thoughts of Aphrodite.

For a while the entertainers withdrew and a proposal was made that each of the guests should tell the company what he considered to be his own most valued quality and possession. A long conversation followed in which a variety of interesting ideas and theories were put forward, lightened occasionally by such remarks as a statement that Homer in the *Iliad* said an onion was a good relish before drinking. Someone thereupon chaffed the newly-married Nikeratos, saying that he meant to go home smelling of onions so that his wife would be convinced that no one had been kissing him. Such flippancy would hardly have appeared in a dialogue written by Plato.

It may have been an hour later when the Syracusan was brought back into the conversation with comments made about the boy and he admitted that he was generally in a state of fear lest some wealthier or more attractive person might wheedle the boy away from him. Talk now passed into a general discussion of beauty and ugliness until the Syracusan began to get jumpy wondering how soon some other turn could be put on for the entertainment of the guests, especially because an argument, not without a touch of acrimony, was beginning to develop among them. Tactfully, Socrates interrupted saying, "As we all want to talk at the same time, now is the moment for us all to sing," and himself started the words and tune in which the company joined.

When they had finished, a potter's wheel was brought in for the dancing-girl on which she was intended to perform some feats of jugglery while the wheel revolved. It was at this point that Socrates made a suggestion to the Syracusan: "I may be," said he, "as you have recently remarked, 'brainy'. Anyhow, it occurs to me that it might be possible for this boy of yours, and the girl too, to exert much less effort and, at the same time, to give us real pleasure in watching them. Now, turning somersaults among knives seems to me a dangerous exhibition, quite out of place at a feast; and it is not really diverting to watch young and beautiful creatures giving their bodies contortions when one would rather contemplate them in repose."

"Socrates," answered the Syracusan, "you are quite right; and I shall put on a spectacle that really will please you." So the Syracusan went off ready to prepare the new episode, while a fresh topic for discussion developed, this time leading up to talk about the difference between what is now termed spiritual and carnal love. The length and form of Socrates' disquisition on all this shows that our author, Xenophon, was familiar with Plato's *Symposium* and was eager to depict Socrates in a rather different light as one capable of regard for and love of womanhood.

Their conversation ended and Autolykos, who was in training, went off to take his usual early morning walk and his father went with him, first turning to Socrates and thanking him for all that he had said.

After he had withdrawn,5 a chair of state, first of all, was set down in the room, and then the Syracusan came in with the announcement: "Gentlemen, Ariadne will now enter the chamber set apart for her and Dionysos; after that, Dionysos, a little flushed with wine drunk at a banquet of the gods, will come to join her; and then they will disport themselves together."

Then, to start proceedings, in came Ariadne, decked as a bride, and took her seat in the chair. Dionysos being still invisible, there was heard Bacchic music played on a flute. Then it was that the company was filled with admiration of the dancing master. For as soon as Ariadne heard the strains, her action was such that every one might have perceived her joy at the sound; and although she did not go to meet Dionysos, nor even rise, yet it was clear that she kept her composure with difficulty. But when Dionysos caught sight of her, he came dancing toward her and in a most loving manner sat himself on her lap, and putting his arms about her gave her a kiss. Her demeanour was all modesty,

5 This and the following paragraph are taken from the translation by Professor O. J. Todd of Xenophon's *Symposium* in the Loeb Classical Library (1922).

and yet she returned his embrace with affection. As the guests beheld it, they kept clapping and crying "encore!" Then when Dionysos arose and gave his hand to Ariadne to rise also, there was presented the impersonation of lovers kissing and caressing each other. The onlookers viewed a Dionysos truly handsome, an Ariadne truly beautiful, not presenting a burlesque but offering genuine kisses with their lips; and they were all raised to a high pitch of enthusiasm as they looked on. For they overheard Dionysos asking her if she loved him, and heard her vowing that she did, so earnestly that not only Dionysos but all the bystanders as well would have taken their oaths in confirmation that the youth and the girl surely felt a mutual affection. For theirs was the appearance not of actors who had been taught their poses but of persons now permitted to satisfy their long-cherished desire. At last, the guests, seeing them in each other's embrace and obviously leaving for bed, those who were unwedded swore that they would take to themselves wives, and those who were already married mounted horse and rode off to their wives that they might enjoy them. As for Socrates and the others who had lingered behind, they went out with Kallias to join Lykaon and his son in their walk.

So broke up the party held that evening.


Symposia—parties like the one just described—were, of course, only occasional events. It was the victory of the boy Autolykos in the Great Games which became the excuse and the occasion for the party described by Xenophon. Our subject is Wine and the effects of wine, one of which can be gaiety. Accordingly, in drawing upon the sketch or dialogue written by Xenophon, it has seemed best to touch only briefly on the solemnities of discussion while laying the main emphasis upon the party's gaiety. Light drinks, good talk and a clever "floor-show" all went to make a long evening and a night of happiness in the hot August weather; for it is fair to assume that Athenian nights, especially with cooling sea-breezes down by Piraeus or Phaleron, could be refreshing in the fifth century B.C. even as they can be now.

A matter of no small interest is that the details of the entertainment given are not in any sense figments of the Athenian author's imagination, but a faithful account of what did go on at such parties. Numerous Attic vases actually painted during the fifth century B.C. show episodes and performers corresponding exactly with those described. Epiktetos, a gifted and brilliant draughtsman, painting on the surface of vases about 500 B.C., produced enchanting scenes on a drinking-cup which itself was once in use in some wealthy household. On the cup's outside was the picture of a symposium, part of which showed a young bearded man in contemplative mood upon a couch beside which stands on the floor a large stemmed drinking-cup; a draped girl, scarf round her hair, plays the double-flutes to him. To the right on a similar couch is an older man, growing bald, whose cup is being filled by a naked boy.[6] Inside the very same cup is a complementary scene showing the same boy and girl (Pl. i). He now plays on her flutes; she has stripped but has a small dappled fawn-skin round her and dances, playing the castanets. One of the contemporaries of Epiktetos was a man known as the Gales painter who decorated the inside of a drinking-cup with a design depicting a youthful reveller on his couch embracing the young flute-girl (Pl. ii).

Twenty years later less formal styles began appearing, for artists were steadily improving their techniques. A man known as the Foundry painter drew a brilliant symposium scene, part of which is shown (Pl. III). Two elderly bald-pated guests, one drinking, one singing, and a young naked girl playing the double-flutes. Though she is wreathed with vine-leaves, she has the short hair-cut of a slave. This is a brillant composition. Of similar date is the picture inside a cup by the Brygos painter. Here a young reveller on his couch is singing while the little flute-girl with her castanets dances (Pl. IV). She is named Kallisto, he Philippos (misspelt), and he holds her flutes.

[6] See *F.R.*, Pl. 73; and Seltman, *Attic Vase Painting*, Pl. 12.

About 400 B.C. other scenes of interest began to appear on Athenian vases. An artist named Polygnotos painted on the shoulder of a large hydria a picture representing young girls practising for a "floor-show" like the one which was described by Xenophon. An instructress is present wearing a long chiton, but the young girls are naked (Pl. V). One, to the left, is balancing on a table, bending her body back and trying to drink from a wine-cup which stands in the middle of the table. The other girl, on the right, dances to the music of the flutes and in front of her are three swords stuck in the ground with points upwards, and she is about to somersault over them. Some ten years later an artist, now labelled the Marlay painter, drew on the surface of a wine-bowl the picture of a boy with a lyre and a

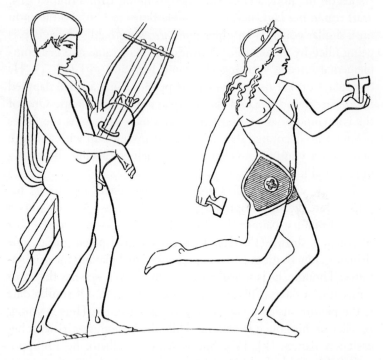

Fig. 1. Drawing after a red figure vase painting by the Marlay painter, c. 430 B.C. Naked dancing girl and boy with lyre. In Leningrad.

dancing-girl with castanets (Fig. 1), both of them reminiscent of the young actors in the *Symposium*. Finally (Pl. VI), we can find on an Athenian vase a picture of Dionysos and Ariadne together on a couch which calls to mind the closing scene of Xenophon's dialogue. This appears on a famous large krater, or mixing-bowl, by the Pronomos painter of about 410 B.C. The rest of the vase is decorated with the most remarkable theatrical rehearsal scene, into which the two principal actors impersonating the god and his bride fit exceptionally well.

There is a certain fascination about the *finale* of the *Symposium* when the two newly-married guests hurry home to their wives. One wonders, of course, what the women may have been up to at home when the men were away at one of their parties. There is no definite record since, if any Athenian woman ever wrote an account of a women's party, it has not survived. Some guesses, helped by recorded monuments, can however be made. But such things must be considered in due course in a later chapter.

*Chapter Two*

❖❖❖❖❖❖❖❖❖❖❖❖❖❖❖❖❖❖❖❖❖❖❖❖❖❖❖❖❖❖❖❖❖❖❖❖❖❖❖❖

# ORIGINS OF WINE

❖❖❖❖❖❖❖❖❖❖❖❖❖❖❖❖❖❖❖❖❖❖❖❖❖❖❖❖❖❖❖❖❖❖❖❖❖❖❖❖

WE have, with the help of Xenophon, been spectators at a very civilised wine-party held in fifth-century Athens, and it now behoves us to ask the kind of question that Socrates, or any enquiring Greek, would have asked. "Where did wine, this happy discovery, come from?" and to add the question, "What god first made this minister of gaiety?"

Conviviality for the average human being is a recurrent need. The well-balanced man or woman also requires a fair amount of solitude to offset gregarious periods of social existence. But young and old, male and female, we like a good deal of company. Yet external aids are clearly required to help people to be natural and gay together and these are best obtained by song, by dance, and by drink. It must be real drink. Tea may be a boon, tomato-juice a medicine, but we need the grape for joy. Much may be done with spirits, and good beer is good food; but it is wine that maketh glad the heart of man. So great has been the social and historical effect of the juice of one particular berry that it is worth enquiring into the origins of the plant on which this berry grows.[1] We will have no truck with freak juices expressed from cowslips or dandelions; elderberries may stay on their bushes,

---

[1] The grape-vine belongs to the botanical family of Vitaceae (*Vitis vinifera*).

14

palm juice turn to rubber. Concoctions are but indecent sub-
stitutes for the reality:

> The Grape that can with Logic absolute
> The Two-and-Seventy jarring Sects confute:
> That subtle Alchemist can in a Trice
> Life's leaden Metal into Gold transmute.

The wild grape-vine appears to have flourished over a well-
wooded territory of no great width from north to south but of
considerable length from east to west, extending from Turkestan,
deep in Asia, along Armenia, the southern slopes of the Caucasus
range, the northern section of Asia Minor, and, as far as Europe
is concerned, well into Thrace.

Evidence fairly recently assembled[2] points to these regions,
and especially to the Caucasus, as the plant's original home.
More than that, the very name "wine" is already present at the
dawn of history. At least as far back as 1500 B.C. the Hittites,
whose language was dominant in Asia Minor and adjoining
regions, referred to it in their cuneiform script as *u̯ii̯an-*, in their
hieroglyphic script as *u̯iānas*, and in a language called Luwian
as *u̯in-*. This is the long-sought oldest cognate of numerous
forms.[3] The discoverers of the Mycenaean Greek Script have
found the word *woi-nē-wei* for "wine-merchant",[4] while the
oldest Greek name on an archaic inscription is "Woinos", which
lost its "w" and became the Classical *oinos*. From this comes the
Etruscan and Latin *vinum*, and all its offshoots like *vino, vin, wein*
and *wine*. The original word was also adopted into other neighbouring languages: *gini* in Armenian, *gvin-i* in Mingrelian, *gvino*
in Georgian. Semitic languages in their turn adopted the same

---

[2] See especially O. Schrader and A. Nehring, *Reallexikon der Indo-
Germanischen Altertumskunde* (1917–29).
[3] H. W. Bailey, "Madu, a Contribution to the History of Wine" in *Silver
Jubilee Volume of the Zinbun-Kagaku-Kenkyusyo* (Kyoto University, 1954),
p. 3.
[4] See M. Ventris and J. Chadwick, *Journal of the Hellenic Society*, Vol. 73,
p. 97.

name for this divine beverage which became *vayin* in Hebrew, *wayn* in Sabaean, and remains as *wa-yn* in Arabic and in Ethiopic to this very day.

Hebrew tradition itself supplies another pointer that marks out the region of Caucasus as the grape-vine's original home, for it is worked into the sequel of the story of the Flood, as told in a part of *Genesis*,[5] which goes back to the time before the Jews went into Babylonian captivity.

When, slowly, the waters subsided after many days, Noah's ark came to rest on the summit of Mount Ararat, highest peak of The Great Caucasus range. "And God spake unto Noah, saying, 'Go forth of the ark, thou, and thy wife, and thy sons, and thy sons' wives with thee. Bring forth with thee every living thing that is with thee, of all flesh, both of fowl, and of cattle, and of every creeping thing that creepeth upon the earth; that they may breed abundantly in the earth, and be fruitful, and multiply upon the earth.' And Noah went forth, and his sons, and his wife, and his sons' wives with him: every beast, every creeping thing, and every fowl, and whatsoever creepeth upon the earth, after their kinds, went forth out of the ark. And Noah builded an altar unto the Lord; and took of every clean beast, and of every clean fowl, and offered burnt offerings on the altar. And the Lord smelled a sweet savour; and the Lord said in his heart, 'I will not again curse the ground any more for man's sake; for the imagination of man's heart is evil from his youth; neither will I again smite any more every thing living, as I have done. While the earth remaineth, seedtime and harvest, and cold and heat, and summer and winter, and day and night shall not cease.' And God blessed Noah and his sons and said unto them, 'Be fruitful, and multiply, and replenish the earth. And the fear of you and the dread of you shall be upon every beast of the earth, and upon every fowl of the air, upon all that moveth upon the earth, and upon all the fishes of the sea; into your hand are they delivered.' And the sons of Noah, that went forth of the ark, were Shem, and Ham, and

5 *Genesis* viii and ix.

Japheth: and Ham is the father of Canaan. These are the three sons of Noah: and of them was the whole earth overspread.

"And Noah began to be an husbandman, and he planted a vineyard: and he drank of the wine, and was drunken; and he was uncovered within his tent. And Ham, the father of Canaan, saw the nakedness of his father, and told his two brethren without. And Shem and Japheth took a garment, and laid it upon both their shoulders, and went backward, and covered the nakedness of their father; and their faces were backward, and they saw not their father's nakedness. And Noah awoke from his wine, and knew what his younger son had done unto him. And he said, 'Cursed be Canaan; a servant of servants shall he be unto his brethren.' And he said, 'Blessed be the Lord God of Shem; and Canaan shall be his servant. God shall enlarge Japheth, and he shall dwell in the tents of Shem; and Canaan shall be his servant.' And Noah lived after the flood three hundred and fifty years: and all the days of Noah were nine hundred and fifty years: and he died."

Mesopotamia was the original home of the story as given in *Genesis* about the Flood which was recorded in the Epic of Gilgamesh, and which seems to have occurred about 2800 B.C.[6] rather earlier than the precise date of 2349 B.C. which the learned Archbishop Usher assigned to it. Another source behind the Hebrew tale brings in Mount Ararat and wine, which are matters irrelevant to Mesopotamian or kindred sources. Wine, indeed, was very important, for, once discovered, it must have gained quickly in popularity among the Bronze-age inhabitants of the regions of Syria and Palestine at much the same time as its use was increasing both among the Minoans and the Mycenaean Greeks. In all probability a kind of wine was already being produced before 3000 B.C. in Mesopotamia.

When Israel came up out of Egypt and prepared to occupy the land which they believed the Lord had promised them, then

---

[6] See André Parrot, *The Flood and Noah's Ark* (S. C. M. Press, 1955), Sir Leonard Woolley (*Myth or Legend*, p. 40), describes evidence for a flood before 5000 B.C. But this was a much earlier one than the Gilgamesh-Noah Flood.

Moses planned to obtain information about the land.7 "And the Lord spake unto Moses, saying, 'Send thou men, that they may search the land of Canaan, which I give unto the children of Israel: of every tribe of their fathers shall ye send a man, every one a ruler among them.' And Moses sent them to spy out the land of Canaan, and said unto them, 'Get you up this way southward, and go up into the mountain; and see the land, what it is; and the people that dwelleth therein, whether they be strong or weak, few or many and what the land is, whether it be fat or lean, whether there be wood therein, or not: and be ye of good courage, and bring of the fruit of the land.' Now the time was the time of the first-ripe grapes. So they went up, and searched the land from the wilderness of Zim unto Rehob, as men come to Hamath. And they came unto the brook of Eshcol, and cut down from thence a branch with one cluster of grapes, and they bare it between two upon a staff. The place was called the brook Eshcol, because of the cluster of grapes which the children of Israel cut down from thence. And they returned from searching of the land after forty days. And they told him (Moses), and said, 'We came unto the land whither thou sentest us, and surely it floweth with milk and honey; and this is the fruit of it.'" Here, indeed, was one of the major inducements for the conquest of the country of the Canaanites.

For all its fertile patches Palestine was a land in which surface water might be tainted and where large areas were parched and waterless. Accordingly travellers must, even in early days, have learnt to carry with them a wine-skin when they went on a journey. A very early story about the destruction of Sodom and Gomorrah beside the Dead Sea illustrates this. Lot, his wife and two daughters, having been warned by the Lord's messengers of the coming annihilation of those offending cities, fled into the mountains.8 Lot's wife—a second disobedient Eve—looked back at the spectacle of divine destructive wrath and was transformed into a pillar of salt; and that left Lot and the two girls. "And Lot

7 *Numbers* xiii.
8 *Genesis* xix.

went up out of Zoar, and dwelt in the mountain, and his two daughters with him; for he feared to dwell in Zoar: and he dwelt in a cave, he and his two daughters. And the first-born said unto the younger, 'Our father is old, and there is not a man in the earth to come in unto us after the manner of all the earth: come, let us make our father drink wine, and we will lie with him, that we may preserve seed of our father.' Thus were both the daughters of Lot with child by their father. And the first-born bare a son, and called his name Moab: the same is the father of the Moabites unto this day. And the younger, she also bare a son, and called his name Benammi: the same is the father of the children of Ammon unto this day."

Such a story would seem to be no more than a piece of political propaganda, designed to smear neighbouring hostile races called Moabites and Ammonites; yet a clever touch of verisimilitude appears in the fact that Lot's family, for all their sudden displacement, had got wine with them. The traveller with wine to hand crops up again many centuries later in the parable of the Good Samaritan,[9] who, on the road from Jerusalem to Jericho, found a man half dead who had been beaten up by a gang, and bound up his wounds, pouring in oil and wine, and set him on his own beast, and brought him to an inn.

Hostility to fermented grape-juice occurs here and there in Holy Writ and has supplied ammunition to sects which commend the intemperate habit of total abstinence from wine. "Wine is a mocker, strong drink is raging", said a writer of Apophthegms[10]; and another[11] declares that "the priest and the prophet have erred through strong drink, they are swallowed up of wine, they are out of the way through strong drink; they err in vision, they stumble in judgment"; and the prophet Hosea,[12] bitterly and briefly, snaps out his doom: "Whoredom and wine and strong

9 *Luke* x, 30.
10 *Proverbs* xx, 1.
11 *Isaiah* xxviii, 7.
12 *Hosea* iv, 11. But all these Hebrew writers were not opposed to wine, but to excess in drinking. For the Rechabites see below, Chapter 10.

drink take away the heart." Such notions do not appear in the New Testament, for the Greek influence within it favours a gentler view, "Drink no longer water, but use a little wine for thy stomach's sake", writes the author of one epistle,[13] while a letter to the Ephesians,[14] merely advises "be not drunk with wine . . . but be filled with the Spirit". Ambiguous, of course, in English, since the words of the Apostle Paul which must displease the vintners might seem to encourage the distillers.

Foreign ways, customs and religions, foreign women and foreign wines were always matters of the greatest interest to Greeks, and it is clear that they took special pleasure in sampling and recording wines tasted abroad. Xenophon—the same who wrote the *Symposium* described in our first chapter—was most famous for that unsurpassed adventure story "The March of the Ten Thousand", also known as the *Anabasis*. Mercenaries from many states were enrolled for an expedition which left the Aegean coasts in 401 B.C. headed for the heart of the Persian Empire. With this army Xenophon went as a volunteer, recording, among other things, the places where men produced wine. The Cilician plain round Tarsus[15] was full of fine trees and vines, rich in wheat and barley. At Damascus he may have sampled a famous wine called Chalybon reserved, normally, for the cellars of the Great King of Persia, as Imperial Tokay was reserved for the Hapsburgs.

In northern Mesopotamia there were villages full of grain and wine; on its eastern fringe the same abundance was found. Kurds on the borders of Media and Armenia had wine in such quantities that they kept it in cemented cisterns. Further to the north-west, above the head-waters of the Tigris, the Greeks billeted themselves in a township where they found, among other good things, old wine with a fine bouquet.[16] The first Greek city reached by the Marchers in the autumn of 400 B.C. was Trapezus on the coast of

---

[13] I *Timothy* v, 23.
[14] *Ephesians* v, 18.
[15] For the wine-god of Tarsus see below, p. 23.
[16] Xenophon, *Anabasis*, i, 2, 23; i, 4, 19; ii, 4, 28; iv, 2, 22; iv, 4, 9.

the Black Sea where they were given abundance of wine. Almost as though in celebration of this the Trapezuntines were striking coins of unusual appearance (Pl. XIV) having on the obverse the portrait of a bearded Greek, and on the reverse the first three letters of the city's name under a table. A pun is intended, for the Greek for "table" is "trapeza". But on the top there is seen a huge bunch of grapes[17] worthy to be slung on the staff of the two spies that Moses sent to smell out the land of Canaan.

Many another Greek on his travels would make similar records, and that is how we know that in the ancient world wine was plentiful not only in most of Anatolia, but especially in Phrygia,[18] Lydia, Caria and Lycia. East of Mesopotamia the grape had very early been grown, gathered and pressed in Iran, Bactria and distant India; and not long after the beginning of the present era it had got as far as China.

People who made the wonderful discovery of wine were bound to attribute it to a god. In fact the god was in the wine; it was his blood; and, with the wine, god entered into you so that for a time you partook of godhead; and that brings up the question "What sort of a god?"

Only when mankind achieves the rare outlook—attainable by so very few—which enables human beings to think of deity in terms of pure spirit, neutral and neuter, utterly remote from matter—only then does man or woman come intellectually to perceive an Ultimate Possible; no Probable, no Certain, no crude Big-man-god. But, since language is employed in the attempt to give the Ultimate Possible reality, language itself breaks back into the vocabulary of the material world. Up comes that which is, of all material things, the most delectable, the most frightening, the most exquisite, the most perfect thing of which man and woman, as highly-tuned hyper-sensitive mammals, are capable—sex. And so mankind which—with few and rare exceptions—must make god in mankind's own image, conceives god or goddess in conformity with ambition and desire.

[17] See Seltman, *A Book of Greek Coins*, No. 113.
[18] Of which more later.

Fig. 2. The peasant God from Ivriz.

Sublimated desire caused the Greeks, and others in the ancient world to interpret deity as a goddess. For a man Demeter filled the mother-need in him; Hera was a type of the wife in whom his pride delighted; Athene was the grey-eyed wise companion of his thoughts; and Aphrodite—whose very name in Greek was used to signify physical desire—was the unattainable dream of loveliness in young womanhood. But for Greek women these god-desses also had their special sense of immanence.

Sublimated ambition caused man to make gods in his own image—gods whom he admired and would above all wish to personate. One man is a simple peasant vintager; another is a market-gardener with vines as one of several crops, a man employing labour; a third is a city vintner owning cellars and a store of varied stocks and brands, which he supplies to the dis-criminating rich. There in Asia Minor we may observe how in each case a man's god of wine becomes a magnified image of what he himself would like to be: a thumping great peasant of a god (Fig. 2), a richly fertile, vegetative, phallic god, or a *bourgeois-gentilhomme* of a god (Fig. 3). Three persons in one god, but they are not really the *same* god, although they are the same idea of

Fig. 3. Two silver coins of Tarsus minted by Satrap Datames (378 to 374 B.C.) representing the local Wine God.

"wine-godliness". As for the women, they too may be found to worship a god of wine; indeed, when in a later chapter we con-sider the arrival of a holy one in Greece, who was to become the Greek Dionysos, we shall observe him receiving from women a more profound, more total devotion than any man ever gave.

Perhaps one should now recapitulate. Asia Minor (often

referred to as Anatolia) is contiguous with the Southern Caucasus, a region where the wild grape, it seems, originated. Once this plant began to be cultivated, it spread at some very early date into Asia Minor, becoming domesticated. Therefore it is here that one may expect to find an early association with an appropriate god or gods, whose cults should survive far into the Greek classical and the Graeco-Roman periods. The types to be sought are three: peasant, gardener and bourgeois. A peasant god (Fig. 2) is a phenomenal figure appearing as a rock-cut effigy, north of the city of Tarsus at a place called Ivriz, near the site of ancient Tyana, where a fertile glen runs far into the northern flank of Mount Taurus. Professor Garstang[19] has described this remarkable sculpture in graphic language.

At the foot of the rock a stream of water, clear and cool, bursts out in tremendous volume, and, supplemented by other similar sources, becomes in a hundred yards a raging and impassable torrent, roaring with a wonderful noise as it foams and leaps over the rocks in its course. Before joining the main stream of the valley it washes at a bend the foot of a bare rock, upon which from the opposite side there may be seen the famous sculptures, the most striking of all known Hittite works, and one of the most imposing monuments of the ancient East.

The treatment of these sculptures is all in relief. In composition there are two persons represented: the Peasant-god, a gigantic figure fourteen feet in height, distinguished by the bunches of grapes and bearded wheat which he holds, and the King-priest, an heroic figure eight feet in height, facing towards the god, with clasped hands raised in adoration or thanksgiving for his bounty.

The god is clad in the short tunic, short-sleeved vest, pointed cap, and shoes with turned-up toes, characteristic of the godlike figures on all Hittite sculptures. But here the sculptor has elaborated his theme, and has worked into it ideas or conceptions which we may reasonably suspect were derived ultimately from the East through the intermediary of Cilicia. The figure is squat and stolid, and the face almost

[19] J. Garstang, *The Life of the Hittites* (1910), pp. 191 ff. and Pl. 57. See also A. B. Cook, *Zeus*, I (1914), p. 594 f. The relief is a work of the neo-Hittites, after *c.* 1200 B.C.

Semitic. . . . Perhaps the most peculiar and Oriental detail is to be found in the horns which decorate the helmet, of which four pairs are visible.

From this view of the peasant god we may pass conveniently to a picture of the bourgeois type, leaving the fertile god of gardens to the last. Geographically there is a definite association, in the corner of Asia Minor where the Taurus range runs into ancient Cilicia, between Ivriz and Tarsus. The big Anatolian god of grapes and corn had nothing of the Greek Dionysos about him. Yet his cult must have been continued far into the period when Greek ideas became dominant in south Asia Minor and in the greatest city of that region—Tarsus. This wealthy and prosperous place was for long the provincial capital and seat of government of the ruling Persian satraps like Pharnabazus, Datames and Mazaeus, all of whom employed its active mint for the issue of silver coins in quantity right down to 334 B.C. when Alexander, on his conquering journey, captured Tarsus and made it one of the master-mints of his own empire. It was in Tarsus that the old Anatolian god lived on in what we have called bourgeois guise. He was clearly a god of fertility, concerning himself with both corn and wine, unlike the Greek Dionysos who left corn entirely to the care of Demeter. But the Hittite god transferred to the coinage of Tarsus (Fig. 3) became a Greek Dionysiac figure. He is seated on a stool, naked to the waist with a cloak wrapped round his legs, holding in his left hand a sceptre resembling a Bacchic thyrsus and carrying in his right hand a big bunch of grapes and an ear of corn. Greek though he is in appearance he is described in Aramaic as Ba'al-tars—"God of Tarsus". This coin was issued by the satrap Datames between 378 and 374 B.C. Later, under the influence of Alexander's coinage which had Zeus as its reverse type, Ba'al-tars became identified with Zeus; but in this earlier issue he is surely to be equated with both the Hittite peasant god and the imported Greek Dionysos. Inevitably when concepts of deity have their roots struck deeply into soil such as that which produces the grape, the belief in them and the presentation of them is bound to last for many centuries.

Dionysos, when he ultimately became domiciled among the Greeks, brought with him and, in his triumphant progress, accumulated a host of polymorphous rowdies: satyrs and nymphs, seilens and maenads, bacchants and thyiads, all of whose goings-on shall profit us later. Among these beings in the wine-god's train three singular individuals stood out. Pan, an ancient god in his own right who would join the riot betimes, was the first. Fat old Seilenos was the second, usually borne in Falstaffian inebriety on the back of a donkey. The third was a mysterious, weird creature, a kind of mystic *daimon* of fertility called Priapos. Explanatory legends of later times proposed to name Dionysos as his father and to make Aphrodite his mother. Others listed Adonis, favourite of the goddess, as the father. That sort of thing, however, must not be taken seriously when one remembers that Adonis is not a proper name at all, but only a label meaning "Lord". Moreover this fitting together of fatherhood and son-ship is only a part of the inborn Greek desire to get things tidied up and properly arranged, since it should be decided who belongs to whom.

One is reminded of the views held by Greek peasants even today about correct relationships. If you are travelling about the countryside in a company of undergraduates, students, or other young people you are careful to arrange your "relationships" beforehand and to stick to them. The girl from Somerville or Girton is your "sister"; or she may be your "first cousin". To be unrelated and travel together is a social impropriety. A young married couple and a single girl go exploring together; the girl had better be the "sister" of one or other of the pair. An older man with younger companions is allowed—like some renaissance cardinal or bishop—a good ration of "nephews" and "nieces".

It is surely with such ideas in mind that Priapos was carefully fitted into the Bacchic *entourage* as a son of Dionysos. Really and more appropriately Priapos might have been his father—or at least his "uncle", for it is very probable that Priapos is much the oldest and most primitive of all Mediterranean wine-gods. Essentially his very name is pre-Greek. "Dionysos", which can be interpreted as "son of Zeus", is a word Indo-European in form; "Priapos"—whether proper name or label—is pre-Greek, echoed in kindred early forms, like the Cretan "Priansos".

Priapos, god of garden and field, had no contact whatsoever with the world of Homer nor with the elaborate theology of Hesiod; that, however, is because they had not come into contact with him. One of the two greatest Ionian cities, Miletus, began to found colonies in the Hellespontine region, which we now refer to as the Dardanelles. There they established cities which grew in importance as time went on; Lampsakos, Parion, and the township of Priapos; moreover other Ionian cities like Phocaea, Erythrae and Paros helped Miletus in building up these colonial foundations. The region where these closely related cities were established was known sometimes as Phrygia Minor or as North Mysia (see map, Fig. 21) which included an ancient township called Perkote. In all these places the principal god was Priapos himself, who was certainly no import from Greek Ionia, who had no connection with Greek Olympian deities, and who was, therefore, a very powerful and tremendously important divine being. If Greeks had not colonised that region they might not have got to know about him and he might have been lost in Anatolian obscurity. As it was his cult was at first disseminated gradually and we can only find evidence for his worship—in a small way— at Athens, Sunium and at Soloi in Cyprus—an Athenian foundation. After Alexander's sudden invasion of Asia Minor and his first great victory at the River Granicus, not far from Lampsakos itself, the army became rather suddenly aware of this almost unknown god of fertility. He astonished them, he delighted them, he became simultaneously important, splendid and an obscene joke. From that moment the cult of Priapos spread rapidly over the Hellenistic, and presently into the Roman world. We, however, in assessing his position as the earliest god of wine, corn and fruits, must distinguish carefully between his local position before the days of Alexander and his almost world-wide popularity in later times, and it is the pre-Alexandrine Priapos who is the more important.

At this point we may turn back in order to take another look at the bearded peasant-god of Ivriz (Fig. 2) with particular reference to his costume which has not always been quite accurately described. Actually this deity appears to wear a long vest, reaching to just above the knees, which has long sleeves each ending in a bracelet-like clasp at the wrist. A belt is worn round the waist. Ankle-boots are also a feature of his *ensemble,* and his headdress calls for special comment. It has been called a helmet, a cap, or a *mitra.* Impossible that it should be the last for there is no sign of the characteristic neck-shield or cheek-straps of a *mitra* such as get tied under the chin. The name helmet raises doubts because it suggests battle-wear for an agricultural god; nor do the things attached to it—eight of them visible—really resemble bulls' horns such as Babylonian gods wore. Boar's tushes were commonly attached to leather conical caps worn by Mycenaean Greeks at a date not much earlier than that of the Ivriz relief, and it is possible that these curved objects represent similar trophies. Our peasant-god wears no cloak, since he is busied with grapes and corn, but the wearing of such a garment naturally occurred, for the so-called King-priest in front of the god has a long cloak hanging from shoulder to ankle. Finally one observes beside the god's right foot something resembling an agricultural implement.

The transformation of so typically Anatolian a god as this one into a classical Hellenic type would be no easy matter, but the citizens of Lampsakos went some little way to achieving it. What occurred may be well illustrated by a little bronze statuette,[20] said to have been found on the site of ancient Lampsakos and made probably about 400 B.C. (Fig. 4). Most statues of Priapos are much later than this date, or are post-Alexandrine copies—often heavily restored—of lost originals. For those reasons our little

[20] Height about 3·1 inches before the feet were broken off. Now in my possession.

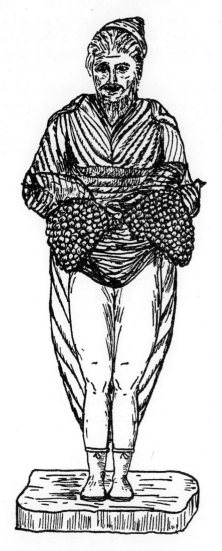

Fig. 4. Bronze statuette of Priapos from Lampsakos. Height 3·1 inches
when complete, fourth century B.C.

figure is remarkably instructive for so small an image. Nothing is missing except the feet, broken off above the ankles; and, as far as these are concerned, it is certain that they were encased in ankle-boots, for other fragmentary examples provide evidence for this fact.

This Priapos wears a long vest, knee-length; but he has caught it up by the hem on either flank to make an apron of it, and in this he displays bunches of grapes, pine cones and an object resembling a small loaf; thus wine and corn are present. Below his pectoral muscles is a belt encircling his tunic. Two brooches fasten a long cloak, nearly ankle-length, which seems to have a hood hanging between his shoulder-blades. The god's spine curves and he leans slightly backwards because of the weights he carries before him: the load of fruits of the earth and of his heavy priapic member. His head-gear is no "turban", as some have supposed, but a loose-fitting cap, of cloth or felt perhaps, having almost the same shape as the cap worn by the Ivriz deity, but without added decoration. There are copies of lost original statues which show that the god sometimes carried in his lap, beside the fruits of the earth, a curved pruning-knife—in fact an agricultural implement.

The whole of this god's garb and appurtenances correspond in a remarkable manner with those of the Anatolian god, and it is hard to avoid the conclusion that the half-Greek Priapos is the same as the Anatolian god of corn and wine. One thing, however, is not represented on the latter, though it is aggressively present on the former—the out-sized genitalia. Greeks were shocked, not by frankness, but by concealment; and, if Lampsacene religious belief declared that the chief deity of the City was impressively phallic, then it was quite essential thus to portray him, lest he take implacable offence. He is, of course, bearded, in which respect he resembles many earlier and later gods; but there is nothing oriental about his features; in fact he has the gentle appearance of a pensive Greek philosopher, despite the fact that the garb worn is most un-Greek in all its details.

Another god of wine caught the imagination of all Hellenic

states, apart from the little Hellespontine group of Lampsakos, Parion, Priapos and Perkote, and that other god—Dionysos— held them in thrall. So the older Anatolian deity never got very far. He may have been worshipped in the island of Imbros whence his cult could have passed to Athens and to Sunium as early as the sixth century B.C. But dominion was already swung by the thyrsus, sceptre of Dionysos; and old Priapos seemed to most men no more than a physically phenomenal follower of a much greater god.

*Chapter Three*

❖❖❖❖❖❖❖❖❖❖❖❖❖❖❖❖❖❖❖❖❖❖❖❖❖❖❖❖❖❖❖❖❖❖❖❖❖❖

# WINE IN THE HEROIC AGE

❖❖❖❖❖❖❖❖❖❖❖❖❖❖❖❖❖❖❖❖❖❖❖❖❖❖❖❖❖❖❖❖❖❖❖❖❖❖

*Iliad* and *Odyssey*, the earliest and greatest of all epics, bubble and sparkle with wine. Vintage, libations, and feasts all convey an atmosphere that is purely Greek. Only the recent discoveries[1] of the Mycenaean Greek Script—which even contains a word for wine-merchant—have enabled us to perceive how much the Homeric and Mycenaean tradition is all a part of the continuity of the Hellenic heritage. Nothing perhaps in Homeric literature tells so much of the full civilised life which the Mycenaean Greeks led as does the long description of the shield of Achilles in the Eighteenth Book of the *Iliad*.

Here is the prelude to the last great climax of the epic. The Trojans, we remember, had pressed the Greeks very hard and were down by the ships beginning to set fire to them when at last Achilles was moved. He had been insulted and his girl had been taken from him by Agamemnon, and he would lift no finger to help the harassed Greeks; yet, in the crisis, he did allow his friend and companion, Patroclus, clad in Achilles' own armour, to sally out and attack the Trojans. Before long Patroclus came face to face with Hector; and their bitter duel resulted in his death. Although the Greeks managed to rescue the corpse of Patroclus, the shining armour that he wore became Hector's trophy and Achilles, unarmed, was unable to fight. At this point Thetis, the

[1] See M. Ventris and J. Chadwick, *loc. cit.*

divine Sea Nymph, mother of Achilles, came to his aid promising
to get for him before the following dawn a new suit of armour
made by Hephaistos himself.[2] On high Olympus she found the
divine Smith in his palace which contained his famous forge and
having promised to comply with her request, he set to work to
produce a suit of armour.

He turned the bellows on the fire and bade them get to work. The
bellows—there were twenty of them—blew on the crucibles and gave
a satisfactory blast of varying force, which increased at critical moments
and subsided at others, according to Hephaestus' requirements and the
stage that the work had reached. He cast imperishable bronze on the
fire, and some tin and precious gold and silver. Then he put a great
anvil on the stand and gripped a strong hammer in one hand and a
pair of tongs in the other.

He began by making a large and powerful shield, adorned all over,
finished with a bright triple rim of gleaming metal, and fitted with a
silver baldric. The shield consisted of five layers, and he decorated the
face of it with a number of designs, executed with consummate skill
and representing, first of all, Earth, Sky and Sea, the indefatigable Sun,
the Moon at the full, and all the Constellations with which the heavens
are crowned, the Pleiads, the Hyads, the great Orion, and the Bear,
nicknamed the Wain, the only constellation which never bathes in
Ocean Stream, but always wheels round in the same place and looks
across at Orion the Hunter with a wary eye.

The story of the bellows working by themselves in obedience to
the will of Hephaistos is remarkable, since it might be interpreted as a prophetic casting forward to the idea of "automa-
tion". Achilles' shield was decorated with zone on zone of
attractive scenes, two beautiful cities—weddings and banquets in
the one, siege and fighting in the other—were displayed.

Next he depicted a large field of soft, rich fallow, which was being
ploughed for the third time. A number of ploughmen were driving
their teams across it to and fro. When they reached the ridge at the end
of the field and had to wheel, a man would come up and hand them a

---

[2] See Seltman, *The Twelve Olympians*, pp. 100 f.

cup of mellow wine. Then they turned back down the furrows and toiled along through the deep fallow soil to reach the other end. The field, though it was made of gold, grew black behind them, as a field does when it is being ploughed. The artist had achieved a miracle.

The next scene was a vineyard laden with grapes. It was beautifully wrought in gold, but the bunches themselves were black and the supporting poles showed up throughout in silver. All round it he ran a ditch of blue enamel and outside that a fence of tin. The vineyard was approached by a single pathway for the pickers' use at vintage time; and the delicious fruit was being carried off in baskets by merry lads and girls, with whom there was a boy singing the lovely song of Linus in a treble voice to the sweet music of his tuneful lyre. They all kept time with him and followed the music and the words with dancing feet.

Next the god depicted a dancing-floor like the one that Daedalus designed in the spacious town of Cnossos for Ariadne of the lovely locks. Youths and marriageable girls were dancing on it with their hands on one another's wrists, the girls in fine linen with lovely garlands on their heads, and the men in closely woven tunics showing the faint gleam of oil, and with daggers of gold hanging from their silver belts. Here they ran lightly round, circling as smoothly on their accomplished feet as the wheel of a potter when he sits and works it with his hands to see if it will spin; and there they ran in lines to meet each other. A large crowd stood round enjoying the delightful dance, with a minstrel among them singing divinely to the lyre, while a couple of acrobats, keeping time with his music, threw cart-wheels in and out among the people.[3]

These scenes, the vineyard and the country dance describe the very things that may be seen in Greece at the present day and in some villages when they dance, the wine goes round until, one by one, the men fall out exhausted. Dances, and harvest time for wine and olives, are the link not only between modern Greece and classical Hellas but between modern Greeks and the men of the heroic age.

Gods and goddesses in Homer are magnifications of the kings and princes, the queens and their daughters who ruled on earth;

[3] Translation by E. V. Rieu for this and the following Homeric passages.

and so, of course, they must have wine like their earthly counterparts. But, the wine of the gods was something more splendid, more nourishing, more potent than anything of which mortals could partake. It was called nektar and was red. Hephaistos is described, in the First Book of the *Iliad*, as bustling through the Olympian Palace of Zeus, handing a cup to his mother, Hera, after which he poured wine to all the other gods from right to left—like the Port at a banquet—ladling the nektar from the bowl, and they feasted all day till the setting of the sun, glorying in the banquet while Apollo and the Muses sang to them. Later, the fourth book opens with a description telling how the gods sat beside Zeus and held their assembly on the golden floor, while in their midst the lady Hebe poured them their nektar and they, with golden goblets, pledged one another and gazed upon the City of the Trojans. Of course any of the younger dwellers on Olympus might find it their turn to pour nektar for the Great Gods: Iris, Nike, Hygieia, and—first and foremost—Ganymede, cup-bearer to Zeus himself.

Mortals and even monsters might compare to nektar a wine in which they delighted, and indeed the giant Cyclops, clamouring to Odysseus for more and more wine, called it a stream of very nektar. In later times the word was frequently employed for wine of choice, quality and taste; and the modern Hellenes, it may be noted, have retained the custom, for when you travel in Greece today you may frequently be surprised to discover on the label of the wine bottle set before you the word "Nektar".

Libation of wine was a part of almost all Greek religious ceremonial both in the heroic age and after. It is a rite and an offering frequently associated with some situation which is tense and emotional, as may be seen from a few chosen passages. Agamemnon had begun the bitter dispute which is the dominant theme of the *Iliad* and which aroused the Wrath of Achilles. In a buccaneering raid on part of the coast of Asia Minor the Greeks had seized the girl Chryseis, daughter of Apollo's priest, whereupon the angry god sent pestilence among the Greeks. King Agamemnon was forced to surrender the girl and, to save his face, demanded from Achilles, Briseis, the girl whom Achilles had captured and with whom he had fallen in love. From these events there sprang the black quarrel which is the *Iliad*'s central theme. But we must consider libations of wine; and, indeed, it was a solemn occasion when Chryseis was returned to her father. With her the Greeks had brought a rich sacrifice which was to be made to the gods.

When they had made their petitions and scattered the grain, they first drew back the animals' heads, slit their throats and flayed them. Then they cut out slices from the thighs, wrapped them in folds of fat and laid raw meat above them. These pieces the old priest burnt on the faggots, while he sprinkled red wine over the flames and the young men gathered round him with five-pronged forks in their hands. When the thighs were burnt up and they had tasted the inner parts, they carved the rest into small pieces, pierced them with skewers, roasted them thoroughly, and drew them all off.

Their work done and the meal prepared, they fell to with a good will on the feast, in which all had equal shares. When their thirst and hunger were satisfied, the stewards filled the mixing-bowls to the brim with wine, and after first pouring out a few drops in each man's cup, served the whole company.

Here is the threefold use of wine; first the solemn libation which goes with the sacrifice. Second, the few drops poured into each man's cup so that he may spill them on the ground making his own libation and, thirdly, the brimming cups from which they drank.

Later in the story there occurs the situation in which—commonsense prevailing—Greeks and Trojans have agreed to settle the war by single combat—a duel between Menelaus and Paris; in fact, between Helen's two husbands, the Spartan and the Trojan. Mortals did not foresee that the gods would thwart this sensible plan and that the war and slaughter would go on. But preparation was made for this most solemn occasion—an armistice.

Heralds, meanwhile, were bringing through the town the wherewithal for the treaty of peace, two sheep and a goatskin bottle full of mellow wine, the fruit of the soil. The herald Idaeus, who carried a gleaming bowl and golden cups, came up to the old king and roused him to action. "Up, my lord," he said. "The commanders of the Trojan and Achaean forces are calling for you to come down onto the plain and make a truce. Paris and the warrior Menelaus are going to fight each other with long spears for Helen. The winner is to have the lady, goods and all, while the rest make a treaty of peace, by which we stay in deep-soiled Troy, and the enemy sail home to Argos where the horses graze and to Achaea, land of lovely women."

When they reached the assembled armies, they stepped down from their chariot onto the bountiful earth and walked to a spot midway between the Trojans and Achaeans. King Agamemnon and the resourceful Odysseus rose at once; and stately heralds brought the victims for the sacrifice together, mixed wine in the bowl, and poured some water in the kings' hands. Then they drew wine from the bowl in cups, and as they poured it on the ground they made their petitions to the gods that have been since time began.

Contrasting with this religious solemnity and the great oath, there is a passage in the Sixth Book of the *Iliad*, Hector himself has returned weary from the field of battle and entered the city of Troy where he met his mother Hecuba. Instinctively she urges him first to make a libation to the gods and then to enjoy a good sustaining tonic drink:

" Wait a moment while I fetch you some mellow wine, so that you may first make a libation to Father Zeus and the other immortals and then, if you like, enjoy a drink yourself. Wine is a great comfort to a weary man; and you must be exhausted after fighting so hard for your dear ones."

A fourth example of prayer and libation links on to the episode at the very beginning of this chapter when Achilles allowed his friend and companion, Patroclus, to fight the Trojans. Achilles went off to his hut and, lifting the lid of a beautiful chest, took from it a gleaming cup from which no other man was allowed to drink the sparkling wine and which he himself used for libations to no other god but Father Zeus.

He took it from the chest, and after fumigating it with sulphur, rinsed it in a rill of fresh water, washed his hands and drew some sparkling wine. Then he went to the middle of the forecourt to pray and looked up into the sky as he poured out the wine, watched all the time by thunder-loving Zeus. "Lord Zeus," he began, "Dodonean, Pelasgian Zeus; you that live far away and rule over wintry Dodona, surrounded by your prophets the Helli, who leave their feet unwashed and sleep on the ground; you listened when I prayed to you before, and you showed your regard for me by striking a mighty blow at the Achaean army. Grant me another wish. I am sending my comrade with many of the Myrmidons into the field. Bless him with victory, all-seeing Zeus, and fill his heart with daring. And directly he has swept the tumult and the fighting from the ships, let him come back to me, here at my own ships, safe and sound with all his armour and his men-at-arms."

Zeus the Counsellor heard Achilles' prayer and granted him half of it but not the rest.

Fifth among the stories of libation we may set one of the most grisly episodes of all. It is the account, in the Twenty-third Book of the *Iliad*, of the funeral of Patroclus and Homer himself—chary of comment—says that Achilles did an evil thing.

They made a pyre a hundred feet in length and breadth, and with sorrowful hearts laid the corpse on top. At the foot of the pyre they flayed and prepared many well-fed sheep and shambling cattle with crooked horns. The great-hearted Achilles, taking fat from all of them, covered the corpse with it from head to foot, and then piled the flayed carcasses round Patroclus. To these he added some two-handled jars of honey and oil, leaning them against the bier; and in his zeal he cast on the pyre four high-necked horses, groaning aloud as he did so. The dead lord had kept nine dogs as pets. Achilles slit the throats of two and threw them on the pyre. Then he went on to do an evil thing —he put a dozen brave men, the sons of noble Trojans, to the sword, and set the pyre alight so that the pitiless flames might feed on them. This done, he gave a groan and spoke once more to his beloved friend: "All hail from me, Patroclus, in the very Halls of Hades! I am keeping all the promises I made you. Twelve gallant Trojans, sons of noblemen, will be consumed by the same fire as you."

The pyre refused to kindle. But a remedy suggested itself to the swift and excellent Achilles. Standing clear of the pyre, he prayed and offered splendid offerings to the two winds, Boreas of the North and Zephyr of the Western Gale. He made them rich libations from a golden cup and implored them to come so that the wood might kindle readily and the bodies quickly be cremated. Iris heard his prayers and sped off to convey his message to the Winds, who had all sat down together to a banquet in the draughty house of the Western Gale. Iris came running up, and when they saw her standing on the stone threshold, they all leapt to their feet and each invited her to come and sit beside him. But she excused herself, and went on to deliver her message, "I have a message from Achilles for you, Boreas and the Western Gale. He is praying to you and promising you splendid offerings if you will come and kindle the pyre under the body of Patroclus, for whom the whole Achaean army is mourning."

And the two Winds rose uproariously, driving the clouds before them. In a moment they were out at sea, blowing hard and raising billows with their noisy breath. When they came to the deep-soiled land of Troy, they fell upon the funeral pile and the fire blazed up with a terrific roar. Howling round the pyre they helped each other all night long to fan the flames; and all night long the swift Achilles, using a two-handled cup which he replenished from a golden mixing-bowl, poured out libations, drenched the earth with wine, and called on the spirit of the unhappy Patroclus. As a father weeps when he is burning the bones of a son who has died on his wedding-day and left his stricken parents in despair, Achilles wept as he burned his comrade's bones, moving round the pyre on leaden feet with many a deep groan.

It was customary in the Victorian and even in the Edwardian era to glamorise ancient Greeks, and among them especially the heroes of Homer, the enlightened politicians and the brilliant philosophers of the full classical age. Achilles and Hector, Pericles and Demosthenes, Plato and Aristotle—those were the names, and for ever will be while civilisation endures. But men who were enraptured by the sublime and tragic Achilles were, in honesty, driven to concede that, Greek though he might be, there was a touch of the barbaric about him. Twelve lusty Trojan captive soldiers, prisoners of war, he sacrificed—their bodies flung onto the monster funeral pyre that was to consume the corpse of his friend Patroclus.

Extravagant behaviour and barbaric! Yet that is only a facet of human nature. Man's occasional desire for human sacrifice seems to rise bubble-wise from the murky hollows of the mind. Among the Aztecs a whole culture collapsed because *un-sacrificed* members of the nation were insufficient politically and economically to keep their strange Mexican culture alive. Overwhelming emotion is always a dangerous thing that may at any moment demand sacrifice by the shedding of human blood as the supreme rite.

Set against the backcloth of the huge panorama of history the behaviour of Achilles and of other Greek individuals and states when the blood-lust was upon them, seems small and insignificant as compared with brutalities such as have occurred in the western world since ancient times. Outstanding are the misdeeds perpetrated at the instance of the Church with the co-operation of the Northern French nobles against the Cathars.[4] It was in that age which it is now the fashion to call the "glorious thirteenth century" that the wholesale massacres of those people in the south of France took place. At least one hundred thousand men, women and children were victims in one city alone of the great blood-bath in the land of Languedoc. Terrible as was the slaughter during the Thirty Years War in the seventeenth century and in the French Revolution as well as in the Bolshevist Revolution in Russia, nothing has occurred between the Crusade proclaimed by the Pope Innocent III against the Cathars and Adolf Hitler's massacre of the Jews at Auschwitz of equal dimensions. Such events emphasise the deep and secret wish for bloodshed that is innate in humanity. One substitute, and only one, has been found: wine. Red wine, of course. In a later chapter we shall have something to say about the Dionysiac, Bacchic cult which came to Greece. After the Homeric age followers of the god Dionysos, though they still went after the blood of young animals, seem, more and more, to have used wine as a surrogate for blood. But it was the simple Christian religion as established

4 See Steven Runciman, *The Medieval Manichee* (1947).

by Jesus in Palestine that first made this rite into something of true holiness.

The use of wine for libation in the Heroic age has so far been discussed by means of citations from the *Iliad*; but there is one important and interesting passage to be found in the *Odyssey* in the Thirteenth Book near the beginning. Odysseus has been regally entertained by King Alcinous who reigned—so the classical Greeks thought—in Corcyra, and the hero was ready to depart when he spoke as follows:

"Lord Alcinous, my most worshipful prince, make your drink-offerings now and see me safely off. And may every blessing be yours! For now my dearest wish has been fulfilled." King Alcinous called to his squire. "Pontonous," he said, "mix a bowl of wine and serve everyone in the hall so that we can make a drink-offering to Father Zeus before seeing our visitor off to the land of his birth." Pontonous mixed the mellow wine, went his rounds and served each of the guests, who then made libations to the blessed gods that live in the far-flung heavens. All remained seated for this ritual except the gallant Odysseus, who rose from his chair, put his two-handled beaker in Arete's hands, and made her this cordial adieu: "My Queen, here's fortune all your life, until man's common lot, old age and death, comes on you! I take my leave of you now. May your house be blessed, and may you be happy in your children, your people, and Alcinous your king!"[5]

In the heroic age there seems to have been an occasional custom of taking wine as an aperitif before a meal starts. Athene, in the First Book of the *Odyssey*, having disguised herself as the chieftain Mentes, comes to the palace of Odysseus to find Telemachus and to urge him to travel in search of news about his father.

She found the insolent Suitors sitting in front of the door on the hides of oxen they themselves had slaughtered, and playing draughts, while their squires and pages were busy round them, the squires blending wine and water in the mixing-bowls.

Towards the end of the epic as the story builds up to the

5 Translation by E. V. Rieu.

stringing of the great bow of Odysseus, the crisis occurs when the suitors, one by one, are to make an attempt to use the bow.

Antinous, in his persuasive way, proposed that they should all take their turn, working from left to right, the way the wine went round. This was agreed, with the result that the first man to get up was Leodes son of Oenops, who used to officiate at their sacrifices and always sat by the great wine-bowl in the far corner. Unlike the rest, be abhorred violence, and their conduct filled him with indignation. Rising now to take the first turn, he picked up the bow and arrow, took his stand on the threshold and addressed himself to the bow. But long before he could string it, the effort of bending it tired out his delicate, unhardened hands.

Leodes, it seems, had assumed the rôle of butler to the suitors, quite naturally since he was the son of Oenops, the Vintner.

Wine was taken constantly with meals then as now; and we need do no more than note two references in the Homeric epics. In the Fourth Book of the *Iliad*, King Agamemnon was reviewing the Greek army and conversing with various leaders of batallions when he met Idomeneus.

"Idomeneus," he said, "of all my horse-loving Danaans there is not one I count on more than you, not only on the battlefield but off it. I show you this when we sit down to dine and the sparkling wine of the elders is mixed in the bowl for our best men. When the rest of the long-haired Achaeans have drunk up their portion, your cup stands full, like mine, to drink from as you wish. Off with you into battle, and be the man you have always claimed to be!"

In the Fourth Book of the *Odyssey* there occurs an episode of some interest relating to life in ancient Sparta in the reign of King Menelaus back from Troy whom Telemachus, son of Odysseus, is visiting. A feast to which the local worthies have been invited has been planned but they bring their own provender, meat and wine and bread.

During this talk of theirs, the guests began to arrive at the great king's palace. They drove up their own sheep and brought the wine that was to make them merry, while their bread was sent in for them by their buxom wives. This was how they prepared for their banquet in Menelaus' hall.

Of all feasts the most interesting is in the Eleventh Book of the *Iliad*, the feast at which that famous and splendid old man, Nestor, was host after he had returned from showing himself in battle against the Trojans. He and Machaon—surgeon and physician, son of Asklepios—stepped down from their chariot and moved to the hut where they sat down on comfortable chairs.

A punch was prepared for them by the lady Hekamede, whom the old man had had from Tenedos when Achilles sacked the place. She was a daughter of the great-hearted Arsinous, and had been picked out for him by the Achaeans as a tribute to their ablest counsellor. She began by moving up to them a handsome polished table with enamelled legs. On this she put a bronze dish, an onion to eat as a relish with the drink, some yellow honey, and sacred barley-meal; and beside these a magnificent beaker adorned with golden studs, which the old man had brought from home. It had four handles. Each was supported by two legs; and on top of each, facing one another, a pair of golden doves were feeding. Anyone else would have found it difficult to shift the beaker from the table when it was full, but Nestor, old as he was, could lift it without trouble. In this cup, their comely attendant mixed them the punch with Pramnian wine, and after making it ready by grating into it some goat's milk cheese with a bronze grater and sprinkling white barley on top, she invited them to drink, which they did.

Two matters for consideration arise from this passage: first, the wine, second, the cup from which the wine was drunk. Pramnian is an intriguing word which occurs once again, but in the *Odyssey* in that episode where Circe had lured into her palace most of the companions of Odysseus with a view to working her magic upon them.

Circe ushered the rest into her hall, gave them settles and chairs to sit on, and then prepared them a mixture of cheese, barley-meal, and yellow honey flavoured with Pramnian wine. But into this dish she introduced a powerful drug, to make them lose all memory of their native land.

One later authority tells us that Pramnian wine came from Lesbos, another that it came from the Ionian mainland near Smyrna. It is a guess, but no more, that it might have been a kind of muscatel. Henderson, however, an authority deserving of respect whose book appeared early in the nineteenth century, had other views about Pramnian, for he claims that "we shall not err much, if we compare it to our common Port wine. It was neither sweet nor thick, but austere, and remarkably potent and durable; in all which particulars it perfectly resembled the modern growth, to which I have ventured to assimilate it. Like Port, too, it was much commended for its medicinal uses."[6] Pramnian was obviously popular for mixtures. There is in Nestor's party something strangely like a modern entertainment in which *entremets* are taken with the punch and we observe an onion—presumably a spring-onion—some kind of sweet, and biscuits of barley meal to be eaten with the drink. Apart from the Pramnian there is not much indication to tell us where the wine came from in Homeric days. A passage in the Third Book of the *Iliad* does indicate that the country bordering on Troy itself produced the grape, for old Priam talks of Phrygia as "the land of vines".

Lemnos was the island from which Greeks who took part in the Trojan war drew their supplies. In the Seventh Book of the *Iliad*, Homer tells that

a number of ships had put in from Lemnos with cargoes of wine—they came from Euneus, the son whom Hypsipyle had borne to Jason the great Captain, and he had included a thousand gallons in the consignment as a special gift for the Atreidae, Agamemnon and Menelaus. From these, the long-haired Achaeans now supplied themselves with wine, some in exchange for bronze, some for gleaming iron, others for hides or live cattle, others again for slaves. It was a sumptuous meal they sat down to.

Wine sent to the war by the son of Jason must have come from grapes grown in the land of Thessaly where Jason and his family reigned.

[6] A. Henderson, *The History of Ancient and Modern Wines* (London, 1824), p. 75.

Nestor's cup, in which the punch was mixed, appears to have been a most extraordinary beaker. Four handles, each supported by two legs; and on top of each, facing one another, a pair of golden doves feeding. Such a description hardly made sense and mystified many a reader for many centuries. Modern archaeologists, one might expect, would be the first to take a keen interest in the shapes, materials and uses of such drinking-vessels as were employed in the Heroic Age and as were mentioned with some frequency by Homer. Actually, however, the interest in such things goes back a long way, for two millennia ago a certain Greek writer named Asklepiades of Myrlea wrote a whole book on the single topic of the *Cup of Nestor* described in the Eleventh Book of the *Iliad*. A certain metal worker named Apelles also produced an ingenious drawing whereby he attempted to explain the position of the four handles with which Nestor's cup was alleged to have been equipped. In actual fact, of course, the whole problem was solved in a relatively simple manner when Schliemann, excavating at Mycenae, discovered in one of the celebrated shaft-graves, the delightful golden beaker which is nowadays always referred to as the cup of Nestor (Plate VII).[7] Homer, it seems, permitted himself a certain poetic exaggeration, instead of four handles each separated by two legs, there are two handles each separated by one leg; and, on top of each, facing one another, there are golden doves—two of them on the actual cup itself. It is, of course, conceivable that a beaker could have been made on which the general scheme of the gold cup of Nestor from Mycenae could have been doubled. Yet it is hard to believe that such an object could really have been attractive, whereas the cup which Schliemann found is an object of exceptional charm.

Many other pleasing shapes were used for wine cups both in the Minoan, Mycenaean and Heroic Ages. Gold ones are surprisingly common,[8] silver much rarer, while pottery cups,

[7] See H. Bossert, *The Art of Ancient Crete* (1937), Fig. 148.
[8] See Bossert, *op. cit.*, Figs. 150–159.

beakers, wide drinking-bowls and great vases for mixing wine with water abound.9

Last among the Homeric tales we must recall the grisly story of the Cyclops and his undoing, which is the central theme of the Ninth Book of the *Odyssey*. The hero tells how he and his companions landed on the mountainous island where in hollow caverns the Cyclopes dwelt. Although he and his crew carried an abundance of wine on board, their lack of more solid nourishment obliged them to land.

Now straightway I commanded the rest of my trusty companions
There to remain by the ship and keeping them close to defend her,
Then of the crew of my vessel selecting a dozen, the bravest,
Started; and sweet dark wine in a goatskin bottle we carried.
This was a wine once given by Maro, son of Euanthes,
Priest of Apollo, the god who the city of Ismarus guardeth.
To us Maro gave it, for him and his wife and his child we protected,
Sparing with reverence, since in a dense dark grove was his dwelling
Holy to Phoebus Apollo; and gifts right splendid he gave me:
Talents seven he gave me of gold well wrought in the furnace;
Gave me a mixing-bowl all solid of silver, and lastly
Wine did he give us, decanting it off in a dozen of wine-jars,
Sweet, unmingled, a potion divine; nor knew of it any
Among all the thralls in his house, nor even a woman attendant—
None but himself and his consort dear and the dame of his household.
Now when it happened they drank of this red wine sweet as the honey,
Filling a cup, therewith did he mix full measures of water
Twenty, and out of the bowl came floating an odour of sweetness
Marvellous. Verily then to refuse it was nowise a pleasure!
This was the wine that I bore in a great skin bottle, and viands
Stored in a pouch; for at once in my valiant heart I had boded
Here to encounter a man, a creature with power gigantic,
Savage, and knowing aright no custom of law nor of justice.

So Odysseus and his companions arrived at the cave of the gigantic one-eyed Cyclops and took their fill of the great cheeses which they found before them. In due course he arrived driving

9 *Op. cit.*, Figs. 115 ff.

his sheep before him and closing the entrance to the cave with a huge rock. He enquired who they were and Odysseus told him of their country and their return from the Trojan war, claiming the while that protection which a suppliant guest expects from a host. But the great brute told him that he cared neither for Zeus nor for any of the immortal gods; and, in the poem, the scene of savagery follows.

Thus did I speak, but with pitiless heart, and answering nothing,
Suddenly making a spring, out-darting his hands on my comrades,
Two in his clutches he seized and as whelps on the floor of the cavern
Dashed—and the brains flowed forth on the floor and the earth was
    bespattered.
Cutting them member from member he straight made ready his supper;
Then as a mountain lion he ate, not leaving a morsel,
All the intestines, all of the flesh and the bones with the marrow.
Meantime weeping to Zeus we upraised our hands in entreaty,
Seeing the terrible deed; and helpless terror possessed us.
Now when at last he had glutted his monstrous maw to repletion,
Feasting on human flesh and the raw milk drinking thereafter,
Stretching him out in the midst of the flocks he reclined in the
    cavern.

On the following day the grim episode was repeated as the Cyclops devoured two other members of Odysseus' crew. But the hero had meanwhile remembered the wine that they had brought with them and, having discovered a bowl made of ivy wood, he approached the Cyclops with the following speech:

"Cyclops, drink of the wine—since done is your cannibal banquet.
Take it and see what manner of drink I had stowed in my vessel.
Lo, as an offering this was I bringing you, hoping for pity,
Hoping for homeward return; but your rage exceedeth endurance.
Pitiless being!—and how might ever another approach you.
Any of all mankind?—for your deeds are verily lawless."
Thus did I speak, and he took it and drank, and a wonderful pleasure
Felt he in draining the luscious draught; and he asked for another·
"Give me again, if you will! and tell me your name right quickly,
Now straightway! You'll get you a stranger's gift to delight you

Here too beareth the earth, rich giver of grain, for the Cyclops
Juice of the clustering grapes that the rains of heaven do nourish;
Ah but a wine like this is a draught of ambrosial nectar!"
Thus did he speak, and again of the fiery liquor I gave him;
Thrice did I bring it and give it, and thrice in his folly he drained it.[10]

No need to continue. No story in all the Odyssey is better known than this exciting and savage tale. It remains none-the-less a magnificent example of the undoing of a barbarian by means of wine.

Many epithets occur and repeat in the Homeric Epics, each of them having its chosen meaning, its special place, its suitable delicacy for a given use; and these epithets always please the ear. *Thalassa*, that musical word for the sea, is favoured with two in particular: *polyphloisbos*, noisy, and *oinops*, wine-dark. Northerners who have not been to Greece, or being there have failed to rise before dawn, are mystified by the last epithet. Yet even quite recently I have watched the sea between Zacynthus and the mainland of Elis from a ship on the way to Katakolo, the port for Pyrgos and Olympia, and have seen a heavy grey mercurial ocean suffused with the purple colour of rich wine as the eastern sun worked its mysterious change.

[10] Translation by H. B. Cotterill.

❖❖❖❖❖❖❖❖❖❖❖❖❖❖❖❖❖❖❖❖❖❖❖❖❖❖❖❖❖❖❖❖❖❖❖❖❖❖❖❖

## Chapter Four

# THE THIRTEENTH GOD

❖❖❖❖❖❖❖❖❖❖❖❖❖❖❖❖❖❖❖❖❖❖❖❖❖❖❖❖❖❖❖❖❖❖❖❖❖❖❖❖

ONCE people have acquired faith in a deity, whether by intellectual conception or by mystical perception, they begin to mythologise. Stories, legends, tales are multiplied and neighbouring peoples, who in their turn have busily been building myths about their gods, are encountered; and what they have invented is seized upon and flung—however inconsistent it be— into the religious stock-pot. No deity in all the realms of religion accumulated so great and fantastic a repertoire of myth as did Dionysos. Yet this seems to have occurred well after the Homeric Age. Compared with the other gods and goddesses of Olympus, playing their dominant rôles in *Iliad* and *Odyssey*, Dionysos has only a very small part. Indeed, the scanty references to him in the two Homeric epics are as odd as they are unexpected. In the Sixth Book of the *Iliad* mention occurs of the powerful but presumptuous Lykourgos who defied a god, chasing the nymphs that nursed Dionysos as well as the god himself who found sanctuary under the salt sea waves where Thetis protected him. Later on, in the Fourteenth Book, there occurs a brief, passing allusion in that remarkable passage in which Zeus, making love to Hera his queen, declares that she delights him more than any of his various mortal mistresses, among whom he mentions Semele, who bore Dionysos. The *Odyssey* contains in the Eleventh Book a vague anecdote about the meeting between the god Dionysos and Princess Ariadne, daughter of Minos. But this story has clearly not attained its later classical form. Finally, in the Twenty-fourth Book, Odysseus tells how the bones of the great Achilles were buried in a great golden urn, a gift from Dionysos.

This vagueness about the god is most peculiar in view of an important fresh discovery. More than once a reference has been made to the recent decipherment of the Bronze-age script (known as linear B), from Mycenaean sites and to the evidence that the Mycenaeans were Greek and spoke Greek. Indeed, these discoveries have inevitably revolutionised our whole attitude to the Homeric Age and its civilisation. Most remarkable, perhaps, is the occurrence of the names of numerous Greek deities inscribed upon these tablets. There exists evidence for Demeter, Zeus, Athena, Poseidon, Hermes, Ares in the guise Enyalios, and Apollo under the name of Paion. Yet the most surprising and the most unexpected name discovered is that of Dionysos appearing unmistakably in the genitive case as *Di(w)onysoio*, followed by a word which could have been either "servant" or "priest". An interesting suggestion has been made that this Mycenaean Dionysos is indeed a god of wine, possibly a primitive Agrarian god associated with the Corn Goddess. If so, this god might be akin to the Hittite Anatolian deity of wine and corn described in the second chapter of this book.[1] Clearly the Homeric Dionysos, son of Semele, would not in those days have taken on the orgiastic character which, in the seventh century, came into Greece with the cult of Thracian Bacchos and his double, Phrygian Sabazios. Mycenaean Greeks had perhaps already a god of wine, though he may not have been numbered among the great gods. Their attitude to these deities is the more remarkable when we realise that they had a single all-embracing word for deity: *Pasitheoi*, "all-gods".[2] Much more evidence will be needed

[1] See p. 24, above. We are considering a possibility for, while the identity of the word is unmistakable, it is not quite certain that a god's name is intended.

[2] On all this see especially Professor V. Ehrenberg, "Griechische Urkunden des Zweiten Jahrtausends v. Chr.", *Historische Zeitschrift*, Heft 180/1, August 1955.

before anyone can assert that the wine-god in those early times was one of the "all-gods". But there was an aspect of his divine personality which, as is gradually becoming evident, prevailed in a remote antiquity when it was believed that he was changed into a bull, and the belief continued down to very late times.

Other gods—two of them at least—might undergo a similar metamorphosis. Zeus, in order to abduct Europa, changed to bovine shape, endeared himself to the girl until she mounted his back, and so swam out to sea ferrying her to Crete, where she became his willing bride.3 Poseidon, elder brother of Zeus, was, at some time, thought of as bull-like. But Dionysos, son of Zeus Almighty, seems also on occasion to have been typified by one of these frightening animals.

At times the head alone of the animal was enough to provide close association with wine. Ceremonial wine drinking and the symbol of the Bull-god are combined pictorially on what is surely the most remarkable of all painted vases ever found in Cyprus: a large amphora which is to be dated approximately to about 900 B.C. Music and formal dancing is the theme on one side of this strange vessel. Five persons are present: four dancing girls and a lyre-player, all naked to the waist, holding or plucking strange flowers like designs on an oriental carpet. The girls wear knee-length skirts and belts, and careless drawing makes the lyre-player appear to be dressed in ill-fitting black tights. These people are evidently performing for the benefit of a distinguished personage who appears on the other side of the vase (Pl. VIII). At the extreme right end the painter has depicted a stylised winged sphinx holding a flower; and this mysterious creature may be interpreted as a kind of attribute of royalty rather than of divinity. One remembers similar creatures, the winged griffins, flanking the Throne of Minos, in the palace of Knossos. But to return to our vase; in the centre on a well-padded armchair-like throne there sits a distinguished lady—queen or princess—of strange appearance. Her legs and feet, seemingly clad in long black stockings, hover over a footstool

3 C. Seltman, *Greek Coins*, 2, p. 170; and Pls. 36, 9, 10; 37, 2, 3, 4.

and she wears a transparent apron-like skirt. But like the dancers on the other side of the vase and like the young woman who waits upon the queen, she is naked from the waist upwards. Immediately in front of her is a little table upon which there stand three little wine jugs, presumably empty. To the left of this is another piece of furniture, a stand constructed to support a pointed wine amphora from which she is about to drink by means of a long syphon which, one may assume, was an elongated reed. Evidence exists for this method of drinking wine on monuments both of Anatolian and Egyptian origin. Still further to the left of our picture the woman in waiting is adding wine to the amphora from a small jug held in her left hand, while, in her right hand, she carries three more small jugs containing further refills for the amphora. Finally, on the extreme left we have a picture of the source, the very vessel from which the wine has been drawn, a Bull's-head firkin, attached to the wall of the room in which this remarkable scene is taking place.[4]

The fascination which bulls exercised even on primitive artists among the dwellers by the shores of the Aegean can be traced back to neolithic times. A small object, but one of the most interesting of objects found in the first year of the American excavations at Olynthus, was a white marble fragment with reddish veins discovered at a depth of 1·25 metres in the neolithic settlement, and possibly made about 3000 B.C. It is part of a vase, or bowl, with a lug shaped as the head of a bull, a unique specimen which is called "a testimony to the high ability of the Olynthian prehistoric stone-cutters". Nearly a thousand years later an ivory cylinder-seal from Crete was engraved with three magnificent bulls, and this was a precursor of many other Minoan seals with such pictures. An intense admiration of bulls, possibly veneration of them, grew apace in Crete, because they were somehow linked with the god of wine.

Evidence at our disposal indicates that a kind of acme of the depiction of bulls in art was reached during the first half of the

4 For full details see P. Dikaios, "An Iron Age painted Amphora in the Cyprus Museum" in *B.S.A.*, XXXVII (1936–37), pp. 56 ff.

fifteenth century B.C.; for it was then that Minoan artists produced certain curious objects which served apparently as firkins, or decanters. They were also—as works of art—much sought after by great personages in Crete itself, in Egypt, and in the Peloponnesus. These were the so-called Bull's-head Rhytons. From the fifteenth century onwards these handsome objects continued to be employed, and the painted scene from Cyprus, described above, shows one in use as late as about 900 B.C. Proof of the extent of their popularity is: first, the famous (though incomplete) black bull's head from Knossos; second, several paintings in the tombs of great Egyptian nobles of the reign of Thothmes III; and third, some very small fragments—a horn-socket here, and an ear or a dewlap there—of six other bulls' heads. To these must be added another, more complete than the celebrated black bull's head from the Little Palace at Knossos.

This head of dark, olive-green, mottled steatite, formed part of a collection of Egyptian antiquities made during the nineteenth century by a French amateur archaeologist who did not appear to have owned any Greek things and there is, therefore, some probability that it was found in Egypt.5 All such heads had in the lower lip an opening from which wine could escape in a thin stream (Pl. IX).

Directly descended from these superb Minoan works of art— which were made not only in stone but also in silver and gold— are great numbers of animal-head vases constructed during many subsequent centuries to act as wine containers, wine pourers, wine filters. Wine running from the mouth of a creature's head is a symbol of its blood, and by such a motif we are inevitably brought round to face the problem of Bacchic passion, the agony of Dionysiac frenzy, the madness in which animals were torn to pieces. The thirteenth Olympian deity was a god of terror as well as delight. But there was a value in these strange manifestations for one of the greatest virtues of Bacchic ecstasy and *enthousiasmos* was that it enabled people—brilliant people like the Greeks—to

5 For a full description see C. Seltman, "A Minoan Bull's Head", in *Studies Presented to David Moore Robinson*.

escape from too much thinking if such escape was for them an urgent need. In this respect it possessed a certain similarity to such "revealed religions" of the Middle Ages and of our own day as insistently formulate the demand for unquestioning faith and obedience; and the maenad filled with the spirit of Bacchos had much the same feelings as the nun steeped in mysticism. So bold a saying calls for justification. Fortunately there is in existence one of the greatest works of literary art, *The Bacchae* of Euripides, which enables us to understand the greatness of the power of Dionysos to a remarkable, even to an overwhelming degree.

Euripides, in his own way a tragedian as great as Aeschylus and Sophocles, lived through the greater part of the fifth century B.C. Appreciated by some and disliked by others of his countrymen, he left Athens in 408 B.C. and was honourably received at the court of Archelaus, king of Macedon, where he composed by far the greatest of all his dramas, the one which retained the highest degree of popularity in all the ancient world. A study of this work is essential to acquire an understanding of the Dionysiac religion which came to Greece from Phrygia and Thrace by way of Macedon, probably towards the end of the seventh century B.C. The violent form which this religion could assume had become a matter of grave anxiety; but from that time onwards it was gradually controlled during the sixth century B.C. in Athens only some hundred and fifty years before Euripides wrote his play. There can be no doubt that he was thoroughly familiar with the historical aspect of the danger.

When the mystical, hysterical, Bacchic religion suddenly struck at quiet sophisticated seventh-century Greece, something terrible and terrifying arrived—something which might have disintegrated the most perfect civilisation in the world's history at the very time when civilisation was just attaining its sensitive awareness of intellectual life and intellectual love, and was learning that these *must* be co-existent with physical life and physical love. Orgy and mysticism—the words are interchangeable—came near to disrupting growing Hellenic balance. Whatever we may hold against certain sixth-century politicians, classified as "tyrants", they, by their tact and wisdom, held the pass and saved humanism; not by suppressing the barbaric, but by accepting and engulfing it in a quiet sea of love and law, of reason and religion. To comprehend this fully we must now summarise the drama called the *Bacchae* of Euripides.

## DRAMATIS PERSONAE

DIONYSOS, *son of* Zeus *and* Semele, *who is also called* BACCHOS *and*
 BROMIOS (The Boisterous) *and* EUHIOS (*from the mystic cry* "euohi")
CADMUS, *formerly* King of Thebes, *father of* Semele *and of* Agave.
TIRESIAS, *prophet of* Apollo, *a high dignitary of* Thebes.
PENTHEUS, King of Thebes, *son of* Agave *and grandson of* Cadmus.
AGAVE, *daughter of* Cadmus, *mother of* Pentheus.
*An* ATTENDANT, *one of* Pentheus' *bodyguard.*
FIRST MESSENGER.
SECOND MESSENGER.
*Chorus of* Bacchants, *eastern women, followers of* Dionysos.
Guards, Attendants, Maenads.

The scene is laid throughout before the Palace of Pentheus at Thebes. Near the Palace are the royal stables, used by Pentheus as a prison for Dionysos, and the precinct of Semele, an enclosure overgrown with vines, which marks the place where Semele was blasted by the thunderbolt. In the distance Mount Cithaeron.

Dionysos, god of wine, of dancing and of ecstasy, is discovered in a courtyard of the palace at Thebes with women and girls, worshippers whom he has brought with him from Asia Minor. In a long prologue he declares that he will punish the Thebans for failing to recognise his divinity, being the son of the Theban princess, Semele, whose tomb is in the centre background of the stage. He leaves for Mount Cithaeron.

The Chorus in a scene of emotional music and dancing tell the story of Dionysos' birth and of the ritual worship which they practise.

CHORUS: I am come from Asia and sacred Mount Tmolus to perform for Bromios a labour that is sweet and a toil that is not toilsome, doing reverence to the god Bacchos.

55

Who is on the road, who is on the road? Who is within? Let him withdraw, let each man keep his lips in hallowed silence; for I am about to sing to Dionysos the hymns that were ever customary.

Blessed is she, who having the good fortune to know the secret mysteries of the gods, consecrates her life and has her soul filled with the spirit of Bacchos in the holy purification of his mountain revels; who practises the orgy of the great mother Cybele, and brandishing the thyrsus aloft, her head crowned with ivy, serves Dionysos. On, on, Bacchae, you who bring Bromios, the god born of a god, Dionysos, home from the Phrygian hills to the spacious cities of Greece, who bring Bromios.

His mother laboured in the travail pains of his birth amid the winged lightnings of Zeus, and brought him forth from her womb as she perished by the stroke of the thunderbolt; but him Zeus son of Kronos straightway received in a new birth chamber; he hid him in his thigh and fastened him in with golden clasps safe from Hera's sight. And when Fates had brought to fullness the god with the Bull's horns, he gave him birth and garlanded him with garlands of serpents, whence it is that the Maenads entwine in their hair the wild snakes their prey.

Soon shall the whole land go forth to dance, as often as Bromios leads his revellers to the mountains, to the mountains; where abides that host of women driven out by Dionysos from beside their looms and shuttles.

The aged Tiresias, the seer, and Cadmus, formerly King of Thebes, meet in the courtyard dressed as Bacchanals, intending to go to Cithaeron, to dance there in honour of Dionysos together with all the women of Thebes, who have been sent there "dancing mad" by the god.

Pentheus, the reigning King, comes in, angry because he has just been told of the follies of the women, led by what he imagines is a sorcerer from Lydia (he does not know that this person is in fact the god); and he is horrified to find that his grandfather and the seer are mad too. Tiresias in a long speech defends the new rites and urges Pentheus to withdraw his opposition. But Pentheus orders his men to hunt down the stranger and bring him in chains, intending to kill him.

There follows an interlude of song from the Chorus.

CHORUS: O that I might come to Cyprus, Aphrodite's isle, where dwell the Loves who charm the hearts of mortals with their spell, and to the land made fruitful by the streams of the barbarian river with its hundred mouths unfed by rain, where (Macedonian) Pieria, the home of the Muses, is pre-eminent in beauty. The sacred slope of Olympus, take me there, Bromios, Bromios, thou god who leadest on the Bacchanals with the cry of euohi. There are the Graces, there is Desire, and there it is allowed to the Bacchae to perform their mystic rites.

The god, the son of Zeus, rejoices in the feast, and he loves Peace, Bestower of blessings, a goddess who nurtures the young. Alike to the great and to the humble he gives the joys of wine that bring relief from sorrow.

Dionysos is brought in, bound; and in an altercation with Pentheus exasperates him by refusing to withdraw from his position. He is thrust into prison. Dejection of the Chorus at the defeat of their leader ensues and they appeal in song to him to reappear. Suddenly, a voice is heard.

DIONYSOS: *Within. The Chorus answer severally.*
　　　　　　Ho! Hear, hear you my voice, Bacchae, Bacchae?
ONE OF THE CHORUS: What cry is this, whence is this cry of Euhios calling on me?
DIONYSOS: Ho, I call again, I the son of Semele, the son of Zeus.
ANOTHER: Hail, master, master. Come to our company, Bromios, Bromios.
DIONYSOS: Shake the ground, Lady of earthquakes!
ANOTHER: Ah! soon shall the halls of Pentheus fall and be shattered.
ANOTHER: Dionysos is in the halls. Do reverence to him.
ANOTHER: We do him reverence.
ANOTHER: Do you see the stone lintels toppling from their pillars? It is Bromios who will raise the shout of victory from within the house. Cast your trembling bodies to the ground, cast yourselves down, Maenads, (*They cast themselves down. Enter* Dionysos.) for your lord the son of Zeus is turning the halls upside down and approaches in anger.
CHORUS: How gladly I set eyes on thee, forlorn in my loneliness.
DIONYSOS: Were you dispirited, when I was sent within to be cast into the dark dungeons of Pentheus?

CHORUS: Yes, oh yes! Who was there to protect me if thou should'st meet misfortune? But how didst thou escape from the grip of the impious man?

DIONYSOS: I was my own saviour easily, effortless.

CHORUS: But did he not bind thy hands in fettering cords?

DIONYSOS: In this I mocked him, for thinking to bind me he neither touched me nor laid hands on me, but fed on fantasy. Hard by the stalls where he brought me to imprison me he found a Bull, and it was about the knees and hoofs of this he tried to cast his bonds, panting in anger, dripping with sweat and biting his lips; but I sat quietly by and watched the while.

Pentheus re-enters, but before he can try again to secure Dionysos a messenger, a herdsman, comes in with news of the women of Cithaeron.

MESSENGER: I come from seeing the wild Bacchanals, who rushed forth with bare limbs from this land in madness, anxious to tell you and the city, master, what strange things they do and beyond all wonder. I saw three companies of women-revellers, one led by Autonoe, the second by Agave your mother, and the third band by Ino. They were all lying asleep, their limbs flung loose at ease, some leaning their backs on greenery of the pine, others on beds of oak leaves, laying their heads at random on the ground, in all purity, not as you say, drunken with wine and music of the pipe and pursuing their loves in the loneliness of the woods.

And your mother sprang up in the midst of the Bacchae and uttered a cry, that they should rouse themselves from sleep, as soon as she heard the lowing of the horned oxen. And they cast deep sleep from their eyes and leapt upright, a marvel of good order to behold, young, old and maidens yet unwedded. And first they let their hair flow loose over their shoulders, and all whose knotted waistbands had been unfastened girt up their fawn-skins and girdled the dappled hides with snakes which licked their cheeks the while. And they took in their arms gazelles or wild wolf-cubs and gave them suck of their own white milk, all who had left lately-born babes in their homes so that their breasts were still full; and they wreathed their heads with garlands of ivy and oak and flowering bryony. And one taking a thyrsus struck the rock, and there issued from it a spring of water clear as dew. Another thrust her wand into the ground, and there the god made a fount of wine gush forth. And any that had desire for a white draught scraped the earth with their finger-tips and found abundant store of milk; and from the ivy-wreathed thyrsus sweet streams of honey dripped. So that had you been there and seen these sights, you would have besought with prayer the god whom you now curse.

The mountain and the wild beasts joined with them in their ecstasy, and nothing remained unstirred by their wild motion. But Agave chanced to be near me as she danced, and I broke from the ambush where we lay in hiding, and leapt forth, meaning to seize her. But she cried out, "See, my swift hounds, we are hunted by these men; but follow me, follow and the thyrsus in your hands be your weapon." So we took to flight and saved ourselves from being torn to pieces by the Bacchantes, while they weaponless swept down upon the oxen at pasture on the green grass. Then might you see one holding a heifer with swollen udders as it bellowed helpless in her hands, and others were rending steers in pieces. Bulls that had before been proud with anger in their horns were pulled to the ground, dragged down by unnumbered maiden hands. And they returned to the place whence they had started, to those fountains which the god had made to flow for them; and they washed off the blood and snakes licked clean with their tongues the stains upon their cheeks. Therefore, master, receive in your city this god, be he who he may, for he is mighty in many things, and above all, they say, so I hear, that it was he who made a gift to men of the wine that assuages grief. And without wine there can be no love any more, or any other of the things that give men joy.

Pentheus is further enraged and promises to call out his soldiers against the women, but Dionysos begins suddenly to hypnotise him into doing his will, persuading him to go out himself in woman's dress and spy upon the revellers. The Chorus sing a lovely song in which they mingle poetry with strange ethics, about the religion of ecstacy and mysticism. Then Dionysos brings Pentheus back dressed as a woman and now enslaved to his will.

PENTHEUS: Lo! I seem to see two suns, and Thebes and the seven-gated citadel twofold; and you seem a Bull leading the way for me, with horns grown out upon your head. Can it be that you were a beast before? For you have become a Bull now.

After a very sinister scene the god takes him off to the mountain, calling upon Agave and her sisters to do their work. The Chorus sing a short song of revenge calling on Justice to kill him, and in that song occur the words:

Reveal thyself as a Bull, or a snake of many heads for us to see, or a flaming lion for us to behold. Arise, Bacchos, with smiling face cast the fatal toils upon this hunter of the Bacchantes as he falls into the hands of the company of Maenads.

There is an interlude before there enters Pentheus' own attendant overcome with grief and bringing the news that Pentheus is dead. He tells how they went to the mountain, and how Pentheus asked "the stranger" (Dionysos) if he could help him to a loftier view of the doings of the Bacchantes. Dionysos pulls the branch of a tree to the ground and sets him upon it. He then betrays him to the women, who, in their frenzy, imagining him to be a beast of prey, pull him down and tear him to pieces.

The Chorus dance a savage dance, singing in honour of their god and his revenge. Suddenly they hear the beat of a drum drawing nearer, ever nearer, from Cithaeron, and Agave now enters carrying the head of her son, which she thinks is the head of a lion. She calls for her father and son to witness her triumph.

Cadmus then enters with the body of Pentheus borne on a litter. After a short interchange with Agave he gradually, in a scene of great dramatic power, brings her back to reason.

CADMUS: Alas! If you regain your senses you will sorrow grievously at what you have done; but if you remain till the end in the state wherein you are now, without being fortunate you will not seem to be in misfortune.

AGAVE: What is there here that's not well done, or what has aught of sorrow?

CADMUS: First turn your eyes to the heaven above.

AGAVE: Look, so I do. Why do you bid me gaze upon that?

CADMUS: Does it seem to you the same, or to have suffered some change?

AGAVE: It is brighter than before and more translucent.

CADMUS: And does this ecstasy still cling to your soul?

AGAVE: I do not know what you mean, but I am becoming somehow clear-minded, and changing from my former mood.

CADMUS: Then can you hear things, and give clear answers?

AGAVE: At least I have forgotten the things I said but now, father.

CADMUS: Into what house did you enter at your nuptials?

AGAVE: You gave me in marriage to him who was born, they say, of earth, Echion.

CADMUS: And who was the child born to your husband in his house?

AGAVE: Pentheus, of my union with his father.

CADMUS: Whose head, then, do you hold in your arms?

AGAVE: A lion's, at least so they said who hunted it.

CADMUS: Gaze well upon it, to look is an easy task.

AGAVE: Ah! What do I see? What is this I carry in my hands?

CADMUS: Look steadily on it, and learn more clearly what it is.

AGAVE: I see a great sorrow, unhappy I.

CADMUS: Does it seem like a lion now?

AGAVE: No, but I hold the head of Pentheus to my misery.

"Dionysos ruined us; I see it now", she cries, and the god appears to prove his divinity over them. The play ends with the parting of father and daughter, the god remaining with his worshippers in command of the palace of Thebes.

This powerful drama—the last work of Euripides who is known to have written ninety-two plays—has tempted translators more than most ancient tragedies,[6] and this is in part due to the fact that the dramatist, though by then an old man, profited immeasurably from his transfer to a country like Macedon and to the court of a king like Archelaus. An exhausted, war-obsessed Athens was left behind for the fresh brilliance and liberty of the slopes of Mount Olympus. The old man, like Tiresias in the play, seemed to regain his youth and "the stimulus of new air and scenery is felt at work in the vividness of many lines describing the power and mystery of mountain solitudes".[7] But what he

[6] The most recent translation is an excellent one by Philip Vellacott, *Euripides, The Bacchae and other Plays* (Penguin Classics, L 44; 1954), with a good introduction. A good acting edition is that of D. W. Lucas, *The Bacchae of Euripides* (Bowes and Bowes, 1930–55), last employed when the play was performed by members of Cambridge University in 1956.

[7] P. Vellacott, *op. cit.*, p. 24.

wrote was not irrelevant to Athens, nor could he ever have written it without the knowledge that he had of the Dionysiac cult and festivals, as they functioned in fifth-century Attica.[8] There they were well under control, and had been for close on two centuries; but it is likely that he encountered in the north the wild religion of Bromios in all its occasional violence. His grandfather could have told Euripides how in the early days of Peisistratus, wild women from the north—a few possessed men with them—surged into central Greece, Attica, and northern Peloponnesus, bringing the strange new ecstatic, mystic religion of a god of wine with them, claiming that Bacchos-Bromios was the same as Dionysos, a simple god of peasants and vintagers, long established in the land. But these wild creatures intruded with something new, and the religion of Bromios was in fact about to disrupt the sixth-century Greek City States as, a millenium later, the organisation of the Church helped to disrupt the Roman Empire.

The concept of the saviour son of god, despised, imprisoned, chained, broken, killed—and risen again in glory and power—is a concept age-old in the great regions where Europe and Asia meet and merge. And whether with the Egyptians you call him Osiris, or with the ancient Greeks Dionysos Bromios (Boisterous Zeus-born), or with the Byzantine Greeks Christos Pantocrator (Almighty Anointed), the intentions are alike. Female devotees caught up in the mystical worship of such a concept of the Divine responded in similar fashion. Bacchos possessed the maenad on the mountain, and Christ the mystic in the cloister. Simone de Beauvoir[9] has written a penetrating account of such phenomena pointing out that the body may play a smaller or a greater part in the feelings of the mystic towards God. Her effusions are patterned upon those of earthly lovers. In the thirteenth century

---

[8] A brilliant exposition of the play and its background may be found in the work of R. P. Winnington-Ingram, *Euripides and Dionysos* (1948). The article on Euripides in *O.C.D.* is admirable.

[9] *The Second Sex* (London, 1953), Part VI, Chapter III; especially pp. 635 ff.

Blessed Angela of Foligno was contemplating an image of Christ holding St Francis in his arms, He said to her: "Thus shall I hold you embraced, and much more besides, not to be seen with mortal eyes. . . . I shall never leave you if you love me."

Madame Guyon, a French mystic of the early eighteenth century, writes:

Love leaves me no instant of repose. I said to Him: "Oh my beloved, enough, let me go." . . . I long for the love that sends ineffable shivers through the soul, the love that makes me swoon. . . . "O my God, if You caused the most sensual of women to feel what I feel, they would at once give up their false pleasures to enjoy such true delight."

We recall the famous vision of the Spanish St Theresa in the sixteenth century:

The angel held a long golden dart in his hands. From time to time he plunged it into my heart and forced it into my entrails. When he withdrew the dart, it was as if he were going to tear out my entrails, and it left me all inflamed with love divine. . . . I am certain that the pain penetrated my deepest entrails and it seemed as if they were torn when my spiritual spouse withdrew the arrow with which he had penetrated them.

These following texts from the writings of Angela of Foligno are especially significant. Jesus speaks to her thus:

My sweet girl, my daughter, my loved one, my temple. My daughter, my loved one, love me for I love you, much, much more than you can love me. Your whole life: your eating, your drinking, your sleeping, all your life finds favour in my sight. In you I will do great deeds in the eyes of the nations; in you I will be known and in you my name will be praised by many people. My daughter, my sweet spouse, I love you very much.

And again:

My daughter, you who are much more dear to me than I am to you, my delight, the heart of Almighty God is now upon your heart. . . . Almighty God has given much love to you, more than to any woman in this city; he has made you his delight.

In the stigmata is fully achieved the mysterious alchemy that glorifies the flesh, since they are the very presence of divine love, in the form of a bloody anguish. We can readily understand why women are especially concerned with the metamorphosis of the red flow into pure golden flame. They are obsessed with this blood flowing from the side of the King of men. St Catherine of Siena refers to it in most of her letters. Angela of Foligno humbled herself in the contemplation of the heart of Jesus and the open wound in his side. The French seventeenth-century mystic, Margaret Alacoque, quenched her thirst for three hours from the Sacred Heart of Jesus. She was the one who offered to the adoration of the faithful the great red clot, surrounded with the flaming darts of love. That is the emblem which sums up the great feminine dream; from blood to glory through love.[10]

Fig. 5. Limestone drum, 0·84 metres high, from Les Fontaines now at Brussels representing naked Bacchant.

[10] *Op. cit.*, pp. 639 f.

Enough has been set forth to show something of the kinship between mystic and maenad.

Yet the maenad differs because she is of the open air; she dances wildly, naked among the grapes (Fig. 5); or, as Euripides said, the young maenads gave of their own white milk when their breasts were still full (Fig. 6). They are shown—the first on a limestone relief from ancient Gaul—the second on an engraved gem now in Florence.[11]

Fig. 6. Engraved gem in Florence depicting Bacchant milking her own breast into a vase.

One should, of course, use the noun "mystic" as a label for a person who claims to have an intuitional knowledge of ultimate reality and such mystics belong to no special race or religion. They may be Hindus, Buddhists, Moslems, Orthodox Christians, Roman Catholics or Protestants, or they may belong to no specified religion or school of philosophy. Mysticism, it must indeed be emphasised, has nothing whatsoever to do with "Sainthood" even though certain persons officially classed as Saints were mystics.[12]

Of a Bacchant as a Mystic one must understand that she does

[11] A. B. Cook, *Zeus* ii, Figs. 32 and 241.

[12] I am reminded of a remark made to me by a well-known sceptic, who spoke as follows: "Of all the strange phenomena in Mother Church, as we see her today, the strangest", said he, "is canonisation. Privates, corporals, and sergeants of the Church Militant on Earth have the audacity, after carefully considering evidences for recorded Sanctity on Earth to tell the C. in C. in Heaven who is to be promoted to Field Rank. Blasphemy, or just plain impudence, which is it?" The sceptic exaggerated.

not feel; she knows. She knows that for some instant of time she has made contact with the reality of appearance and she may renew this experience from time to time. It is a point that mystical experiences are much more common than is usually believed. They may come to any of us, most especially during adolescence, although no age-group is immune and those who have the experience are not necessarily either eccentric or brilliant people. When it is remembered that in the Greek world each votary was himself or herself Bacchos or Bacche, and so part of god, then we perceive something remotely prefiguring the Quaker belief that there is in every man a spark of divinity, an inward light, a seed, a Christ within.[13]

Bacchos was of such overwhelming importance that, under the mantle of Dionysos, he had to become an Olympian, and therefore the Thirteenth God. Tradition, however, demanded exactly twelve Canonical Olympian gods and so someone had to yield up a place. It was not a question of stepping down, but of retiring into a grey triviality—rather inconsequently, and it was the gentle old-maid goddess Hestia who retired. About the middle of the fifth century B.C. there was carved a marble relief said to have been found in the Greek city of Tarentum. Twelve deities were depicted as moving along in procession and Hestia was one of them. When the Parthenon was completed in 432 B.C., the twelve Olympians were shown on the frieze at the east end. Hestia was missing but Dionysos was present. He had been fitted in.

Long ago Greek myth seems to have handled certain problems that beset the human race and myth could anticipate both psychoanalysis and psychiatry, for Oedipus existed before Freud. If in the ancient world there were human misfits then there could also have been divine misfits, and Dionysos was one. Olympus in the *aither* and Delphi on earth took the god in charge and finished by turning him into a pattern of rather lascivious rectitude. But this phenomenon, together with political aspects of orgy and mysticism must be left for later reflection.

[13] On all this see V. H. Mottram, *The Physical Basis of Personality* (Pelican), pp. 149 ff.

*Chapter Five*

# VINTAGE

ARISTON MEN HYDOR: "Water is best"; the famous three words open the published poems of Pindar, for they stand at the beginning of his First Olympian Ode, written for Hieron, ruler of Syracuse, whose horse won the race at Olympia in 476 B.C. Much comment has been made on the phrase, largely because past scholars, unfamiliar with modern Greece, thought of the ancient Greeks as continuous symposian wine-bibbers.

Oddly enough it was water as often as wine that inspired poets; and there are still springs with famous names to visit: Castalia and Kalliroe at Delphi; Hippocrene of Helicon; on the summit of Acrocorinth, cold Peirene, which gushed forth when the hoof of Pegasus first struck the rock, and a second Peirene, with its elaborate well-house, in the agora of Corinth itself; and Glauke, another spring nearby. In Athens there were at least two named Ennakrounos, or "Nine-Spouts", as well as Klepsydra on the Acropolis. The Greeks of today, it has been often remarked, are as devoted to their water as were the ancients; and, in one respect, the situation has not changed, for you could then, as now, get good wine in variety to suit your palate, though ice-cold gushing water, tasting sharply or smoothly of minerals within the rock, was a rarity to be relished on the spot and not transportable. Artesian wells were, of course, unknown; surface rain-water, which in arid regions was carefully stored in underground cisterns, was bound to contain impurities; and the ordinary well in the plain or valley was, or is, so easily tainted that the ancients, like the moderns, found in most places that wine alone was safe and hygienic. Pindar's enthusiasm for pure water still exists, and the editors of the *Guide Bleu* (1948 edition) comment as follows: "Spring water, often exquisite, is perhaps the commodity that most excites the greed of this abstemious people. They drink great quantities: it is served everywhere in big glasses with ouzo, coffee, or Turkish delight. People drink it by itself, or sometimes mixed with a little wine, and the modern Greek attributes a thousand beneficent virtues to his water. Even the tourist ends by distinguishing the qualities and tastes of different springs"— especially in the mountain regions. The *Guide Bleu*—naturally patronising in its assessment of most modern Greek wines— gives guarded approval to resinated wine (of which more presently), but admits it to be a taste worth acquiring.

Tainted water, and the risk of drinking it, encouraged viti-culture in ancient Greece, and therefore helped trade in wine, the supposed medicinal virtues of which may be gauged by the fact that it was regularly supplied to slaves to keep them in good health.

Something must now be said about the grape-gathering and the conversion of the fruit into wine in ancient times. Where the usual practice of growing well-trenched dwarf-vines prevailed, vintagers would naturally kneel to collect the ripe bunches; and there are terracotta reliefs representing peasants, sometimes posed as though they were tailed satyrs, in the appropriate attitude. The handsomest wine coinage of all, that of Mende, has upon the obverse of its silver coins Dionysos himself, wine-cup in hand, reclining upon the back of a leisurely ass. On the reverse there is a good design (Pl. XIV), a small squat grape-vine with four ripe bunches, the kind of vine one sees today wherever it can live in Greece; and the frame around the vine on the coin suggests its four-square earthy setting. Maronea—the "Bordeaux" of the wine country of Thrace—showed on the reverse of its coinage a dwarf-vine like that of Mende. The rarer type of climbing vine appears on an Attic black-figure vase of about 550 to 540 B.C., now in the Louvre (Fig. 7). The vine trails round the support afforded by an old dead tree-trunk, spreading on to branches which are held up by four stout wooden props. The grapes are being gathered by a number of persons, including several boys of various ages, the youngest of whom have climbed

Fig. 7. Attic black-figure vase painting, c. 550–540 B.C. Peasants and boys collecting grapes from a climbing vine.

aloft into the weakest branches and trailers. A greedy dog takes a lick at an oozing bunch; and two old bearded peasants pack the grapes in baskets. They, like the boys, are naked, and are pictured with hair on their chests—a sign of uncouthness in a country where depilation of chests, arms and legs was fairly general among men of gentle birth. Once gathered, the grapes were flung into a great stone vat to be trodden rhythmically in a kind of dance accompanied by simple music. There is an amusing caricature of the whole vintage business in which satyrs impersonate the peasants. It is on an Attic amphora of about 550 B.C. painted by the Amasis painter (Fig. 7a) who condensed the elaborate process into a single comic picture. Even today the

Fig. 7a. Attic black-figure vase painting by the Amasis painter, *c.* 550 B.C.
The whole process of vintage with Satyrs impersonating peasants.

same method, the rhythm and the musicians with their vintage
melodies exist in Greece. Some of the juice, *gleukos*, was consumed at once, after being clarified with a dash of vinegar; some
of it was placed in cauldrons and simmered to reduce the fluid,
the result being a grape-jelly, *hepsema*. The remaining *gleukos*—
that is, the bulk of the trodden grapes—went into large bell-
mouthed jars, *pithoi*, in which the process of fermentation took
place; and this went on for about nine days, carefully watched so
that the scum on top could be skimmed off. Body was given to
the wine by adding a quantity of sweet *hepsema* before fermentation; and the alcoholic content of the drink would be augmented
according to the amount added. Next the *pithoi* were covered
with lids well rubbed with pine cones, mastic, and other herbs
according to taste, in order to counteract the rum-like sweetness
of the wine. Every thirty-six days the jars were inspected, and

more pine cone flavour was added. It was in the following spring that the best kinds of wine were drawn from the *pithoi*, "bottled", and stoppered in the long pointed wine-amphorae ready for distribution. The interval between bottling and the consumption of the wine varied greatly, according to brand and to personal judgment and taste; and wine merchants carried cellars full. The strong reinforced wines, akin to port and sherry, were safe for keeping; the lighter ones were not, and these were generally treated with resin as a preservative, in which respect the ancient *oinos retinites* closely resembled the Greek *retsina* in constant use today.

An author, busying himself with the study of wine in the ancient world, is asked by his friends one question more frequently than any other: "What did ancient Greek wine taste like?"

His first answer must be: "We do not know." Yet he may add a second answer: "In some cases we can guess, and not too badly." There is said to be, in the museum of a Rhineland city, an ancient clay amphora of Roman Imperial date containing wine imported from the Mediterranean to what is now Western Germany, and this wine may be a Greek or a Graeco-Italian product. Stoppered with a tight seal, it has never been opened, although when shaken liquid can be heard slushing around inside. And it would be useless to open it. Alcohol would have evanesced many centuries ago; colour would have adhered permanently to the inside of the amphora, leaving nothing but stale brackish water. Should an underwater archaeologist ever bring from the bed of the sea a Greek amphora which still contained something liquid, it would be tasteless non-vinous liquid, without any doubt.

Justification for guessing about some kinds of ancient wine is founded in a regard for historical continuity. The first instance concerns that celebrated Byzantine wine produced in Peloponnesus and named after the little Byzantine city from which it first began to be exported—Monemvasia.

This word took on a mediaeval French form as Malvoisie, which became anglicised as Malmsey. Strong and sweet when young it is immensely improved by age. The kind of grapes from which it is made were found to occur in Samos, Crete, Cyprus and many other islands, and, transported to Sicily, their fruit became known as Marsala. Ultimately the same stock, being cultivated in Madeira, attained to the distinction of that famous dessert wine. A like transplating of vine-stocks concerns the sherry of Cadiz and Jerez descended from the vines of Shiraz. We have kept for this superb wine the name of the Persian city. Malmsey which came to England, like the butt-full in which the Duke of Clarence was drowned and like the cask which Erasmus had sent to him in Queens' College, Cambridge, was a Greek wine. We may be confident that it tasted like Madeira not only in Byzantine times but in the ancient world as well. Everything, however, depended upon its being laid down long before it was consumed.

A fortunate experience was mine in the mid-twenties of the present century. Dining with an old friend—the late Senator Petsalis—in Athens, I was given after dinner a superb Samian. My host's grandfather had laid down the cask in 1830, and what we drank had only recently been bottled. Its *bouquet* was a dream, it had the velvet of a great claret and the body of old Madeira. A more pleasing wine has never come my way. But age was a factor of the utmost importance, for if you sample new Samian you will find it harsh and sweet like some public-house "port-wine" with a Madeira tang to it. Indeed most of the abundant vintage of Samos is nowadays pumped into tankers and shipped direct to Madeira where it merges with the local product in the same vats.

In the early part of the last century a most interesting essay on contemporary Greek wine was written by the only authority of that age competent to discuss the topic in English, Mr Alexander Henderson, and it appeared as Chapter VII in Part II of his book, *The History of Ancient and Modern Wines* published in London in 1824, and deserves full quotation. First, however, the appropriateness of his opening paragraph must be explained, for this book of his came out in the very year in which Byron died in the cause of Greek Liberty at Missolonghi. Three years earlier the

War of Liberation began when Archbishop Germanos at Patras raised the blue standard with the white cross and called on the Greeks to revolt. The fearful massacre of Greeks with their Patriarch Gregory in Constantinople, and the subsequent wholesale murder of the inhabitants of Chios—most prosperous of Greek islands—shook the Chancelleries and Churches of Europe. Final liberation was not to come until three years after the book on wine had appeared. But we must turn to Mr Henderson's chapter, short as it is, for it deserves reproduction in full, in fact a new edition.

## OF THE WINES OF GREECE, AND OF THE ISLANDS OF THE ARCHIPELAGO AND IONIAN SEA

When we consider the degrading bondage which the descendants of the ancient Greeks have so long endured, but from which they are now happily emancipating themselves, we can feel no surprise at the decline of that spirit of enterprise and industry, for which their nation was once so pre-eminently distinguished. Wherever the Turkish arms have penetrated, desolation has followed in their train. Lands, which, in former times, yielded the richest harvests, have been suffered to run to waste; whole districts have been abandoned; and the wretched inhabitants who remain, enjoying no security of person or property, after being forced to contribute one-seventh of their crop to a government which is constantly harassing and oppressing them, can look forward to little improvement in their circumstances by increased exertion; and are, therefore, generally content to snatch, by a hasty and imperfect cultivation of the soil, the few productions required for their immediate subsistence. It is only in those islands which have remained longest exempt from the baneful presence of the Turks, or where the Greeks, by the preponderance of their numbers, have been enabled to secure a slight degree of freedom, that agriculture and commerce have made any progress, or, to speak more correctly, have not been altogether neglected. While under the Venetian republic, Candia and Cyprus supplied the whole of Europe with the finest dessert wines, and so abundant was their produce, that, towards the end of the sixteenth century, the former island alone, if we may credit Bacci, sent annually to the shores of the Adriatic not less than two hundred thousand casks of malmseys. (Bacci, *Naturalis Vinorum Historia*, p. 331.) Since it has experienced the miseries attendant on Turkish sway, the Greek population has gradually diminished; the manufacture of wine has been confined to a few districts; and the quantity procured is insufficient to meet the wants of the inhabitants. (*Voyage dans l'Empire Othoman, &c.* par G. A. Oliver. Paris, An VII. Tome I, p. 406.) When Mr Drummond travelled, the average amount of the exportation from Cyprus was estimated at 365,000 *cuse*, or 973,333 gallons, and the total produce of the wine harvest at 800,000 *cuse*, or 2,133,333 gallons. (*Travels through different Cities of Germany, Italy and Greece.*; by Alexander Drummond. London, 1754, p. 156.) About fifteen years ago, the quantity exported was reduced to 65,000 *cuse*; and the supply of common red and white wines for internal consumption was only about as much more. Such is the change effected by the government of the Captain Pacha, in whom the property of this fertile island is now vested!

Throughout nearly the whole of Greece, the soil is highly favourable to the vine. On the continent, the extensive ranges of mountains, which intersect the country, are chiefly calcareous. In those islands which have been celebrated for their general fertility, and the superiority of their wines, at Scio (the Chios of the ancients), Tenedos, Candia, Zante, &c., similar strata occur: in others, where the growths are of equal repute, as Lesbos, Naxos and Santorini (the Thera of the ancients), the rocks are of volcanic origin. The variety of climate and choice exposures, which the elevated grounds present, serves to diversify, to an infinite degree, the quality of the wines obtained; and in many districts the method pursued in the cultivation of the vine must be acknowledged to be far from injudicious. It is cut near the root, and allowed to extend its branches laterally; and in the best vineyards the employment of manure is avoided. Nothing, in short, is wanting to secure a produce equal to that of the Hermitage or of Madeira, but a more skilful treatment of the vintage, and the abandonment of those deleterious admixtures, which, in conformity to long established prejudices, are still very generally resorted to. The grapes, for the most part, are gathered indiscriminately, and thrown into an open cistern, where they are exposed to the full influence of the atmosphere; and, as they are often half-dried before they are trodden, a quantity of water is added to them, in order the facilitate the fermentation. Salt, baked gypsum, and lime, are used to correct the sweetness of the liquor; and a portion of resin is commonly introduced, as in ancient times, to imitate the pungency of old wine. In some places, the product of the fermentation is collected in skins smeared with tar, which impart a disagreeable flavour, and render it unfit for use, until it has been mellowed by long keeping: but the poverty of the farmers will seldom allow them to adopt the proper means for preserving their wines. Hence it comes, that the lighter growths often turn entirely acid in the course of a few months after the vintage; and only the stronger kinds will keep beyond the year. In those situations, however, which have been favoured by commerce, and where subterraneous cellars have been formed, wines of considerable age may be occasionally met with. "The red wine of Ithaca", a late traveller observes, "is excellent, superior to that of Tenedos, the Greek wine which it most resembles; but it is generally much injured, sometimes spoiled, by the injudicious manner in which it is kept. In the possession and management of the British commandants at Cephalonia and Ithaca, we found it a delightful wine, with a Hermitage flavour, and a good sound body." (*Travels in Italy and Greece;* by H. W. Williams, Vol. II, p. 201.)

In the present, as in former times, the best Greek wines are of the luscious-sweet class. Those made in Cyprus and Tenos, the red muscadine of Tenedos, and the white muscadine of Smyrna, vie with the richest Hungarian wines. Several of the islands, however, as Ithaca, Cephalonia, Candia, and Cyprus, yield abundance of dry red wines, which resemble the secondary growths of the

Rhone, and which, with a little more care in manufacture, might be rendered fit for general exportation. Even now a considerable quantity is sent to the ports of the Black Sea. The red wine of Corfu is distinguished by its lightness and delicacy. In the island of Zante a wine is made from the Corinth grape, which is said to approach to Tokay.

Candia and Cyprus alone, if properly cultivated, would be capable of supplying us with every variety of wine. In the former island, the vineyards of Kissanos yield an agreeable claret; while those of Rethymo give a fine-flavoured white wine, which keeps very well; and the malmsey made by the caloyers of Canea, and on the hills adjacent to Mount Ida, has been long in high estimation. In Cyprus, the domain called the *Commendaria*, from its having belonged to the Knights of Malta, affords the choicest sweet wine. When new, it is red; but, as it advances in age, it grows tawny, and improves in delicacy and flavour, till it surpasses almost all the other wines of the Archipelago. The white muscadine of Cyprus[1] is also an excellent dessert wine, but has generally a disagreeable taste of the tar or pitch used for coating the bags in which it is conveyed from the mountains. According to Olivier, however, the white wine of Santorini, known under the name of *vino santo*, ranks before the best growths of Cyprus. It is principally exported to Russia. (*Voyage dans l'Empire Othoman, &c.*, Tome I, p. 361.)

The scarcity of wood in many of the islands has led the natives to use vats of masonry, which, when well made, and kept properly clean, answer the purpose very well. "Every private man", says Tournefort, "has in his vineyard a sort of cistern, of what dimensions he thinks fit; it is made square, well walled, and cemented with brick mortar; open at the top. In this they stamp the grapes, after letting them lie two or three days to dry: as fast as the must runs out at a certain hole of communication into a basin placed below the cistern, they pour it into leathern budgets,

---

[1] The wines of Cyprus have on the whole fallen from grace, and things have been grossly aggravated by a large-scale inthrust of Coca-cola which is spoiling both Orthodox Christians and Moslems (Author).

and carry it to town, where they empty it into casks of wood, or large earthen jars, buried up to the neck in the ground: in these vessels the new wine works as it may; they throw into it three or four handfuls of white lime plaster, with the addition now and then of a fourth part of fresh or salt water. After the wine has sufficiently worked, they stop up the vessels with plaster." (*Voyage into the Levant*, Vol. I, p. 125.)

In most of the islands, the processes adopted in the making of wines are, with few exceptions, the same. In Cyprus, for the best muscadine wines, they twist them on the stalk a short time before they are gathered. "At Scio (Chios)," according to the author last quoted, "they plant their vines on the hills, and cut the grapes in August, and let them lie in the sun to dry for seven or eight days, after which they press them, and then let them stand in tubs to work, the cellar being all the while close shut. When they would make the best wine, they mix among the black grapes a sort of white one which smells like a peach kernel; but in preparing nectar, so called even to this day, they make use of another kind of grape, somewhat styptic, which renders it difficult to swallow. The vineyards most in esteem are those of Mesta, from whence the ancients had their nectar. Mesta is, as it were, the capital of that famous quarter called by the ancients Ariousia." (*Ibid.*, p. 283.)

On the continent of Greece, although there is no want of the finest situations on the slopes of the calcareous mountains that divide the country, the poor peasants are induced, by the temptation of a larger produce, and the saving of labour, to plant their vines on the low lands, which are generally marshy in the winter, and consequently very unpropitious to the finer qualities of the grape. The vintage is collected with little care, and is usually trodden out on platforms in the fields, whence it is conveyed in skins to the towns and villages, to undergo an imperfect, or an excessive fermentation. In order to give the indifferent wine thus obtained a little more body, a large quantity of the resin of the pine-tree is added: but even with this assistance it will hardly keep till the next summer; and during the hot months of the year,

the Greeks seldom drink any thing better than vinegar.[2] In fact,
it is only in this state that the liquor becomes clear: until it is sour,
it is always muddy. In some parts of Macedonia, however, very
tolerable wines are met with. Here are several towns which have
long flourished by their overland traffic with Germany; and many
of the inhabitants, having resided long in that country, have
introduced a better mode of making wine, and the use of subterranean cellars. The climate of the greater part of Macedonia, it
may be observed, is colder than any other southward of the Alps,
and therefore between this province and the Archipelago we
should undoubtedly find abundance of sites capable of producing
every variety of wines to be found in France and Spain. The
Morea no longer affords any but the worst quality, although it is
the original country of the Malvasia or malmsey grape, from
which the sweet wines of Madeira, Malaga, and other places,
derive their name.

So ends Mr Henderson's impressive account of Greek wines as
they were in his own day. His work has helped us to guess at the
quality, and even at the tastes, of wines in antiquity, while, at the
same time, he has supplied a link between wines made in his day
and in ours.

Reference has been made above both to the treading of the
grapes in the remote days of ancient Greece and to the more recent
practice of the early nineteenth century. Today the procedure is
not much different from what antiquity could show. In every
village and district it is known in advance when this or that owner
of a wine-press is going to begin the making of his wine. Long
ago the priest of Dionysos came along with a crude little wooden
image of the god to bless the work. Today it is the village Papas
who comes bearing a little icon of the Virgin Mary, the All-holy
Mother of God. And what deity could be more appropriate than

[2] On my last visit (1956) to Delphi I insisted on sampling the local
resinated wine, which on former occasions I had enjoyed. I was warned that
there had been a bad year. They were right, it was turning to vinegar
(Author).

this one, who caused her Son to perform, almost unwillingly, His first miracle? It is all there in the second chapter of the Gospel according to St John.

"And the third day there was a marriage in Cana of Galilee; and the mother of Jesus was there: and both Jesus was called, and his disciples, to the marriage. And when they wanted wine, the mother of Jesus saith until him, 'They have no wine.' Jesus saith unto her, 'Woman, what have I to do with thee? mine hour is not yet come.' His mother saith unto the servants, 'Whatsoever he saith unto you, do it.' And there were set there six water-pots of stone, after the manner of the purifying of the Jews, containing two or three firkins apiece. Jesus saith unto them, 'Fill the water-pots with water.' And they filled them up to the brim. And he saith unto them, 'Draw out now, and bear unto the President of the feast.' And they bare it. When the President of the feast had tasted the water that was made wine, and knew not whence it was, (but the servants which drew the water knew), the President of the feast called the bridegroom, and saith unto him, 'Every man at the beginning doth set forth good wine; and when men have well drunk, then that which is worse: but thou hast kept the good wine until now.' This beginning of miracles did Jesus in Cana of Galilee, and manifested forth his glory; and his disciples believed on him."

Anyhow there is a ritual to be observed, now as of old, when the first grapes are pressed.

Seven miles out of Athens to the north-east on the low saddle that divides Pentelicus from Hymettus is a little place called Stavros, "Cross-roads", at the fork of the roads to Marathon and Sunium. At Stavros a certain Costa keeps a *taverna* well-known for excellent cooking and for a dry red Markopoulo that can have the quality of a good Beaujolais. Athenians and foreigners with taste would turn in at Costa's for a midday meal knowing that they would not be disappointed. One late summer's day a well-known diplomat, accompanied by his lady, a counsellor and a young American attaché,[3] stopped at the *taverna* where lunch was

3 I owe the story that follows to the young American attaché himself.

served on well-scrubbed tables under the shade of olive trees. Costa remarked to his excellency that he was going to press his grapes on the following Monday, and the guests at once asked if they might come and see. But what an honour for Costa, of course, of course! And so on Monday early in the morning the distinguished strangers arrived, this time in two cars, for his excellency's two children and their Nannie came too to see the fun.

Beside the long low house which adjoined the *taverna* was a great wine-press like some big tank hewn out of the mountain side, which at that point is solid grey Hymettian marble. Spouts drilled into the tank's side were devised to pour the grape-juice into pottery jars placed in readiness below them, and black-skinned grapes were piled high in the press. The village Papas with his holy icon had been, blessed the grapes, and moved on to the house of some other vintager, and Costa awaited his distinguished guests. They left their cars and sat down under the olive-trees where Turkish coffee was served them, with water and Loukoumi for the children. Beside Costa and his wife and growing family were two strangers—musicians, one with a fiddle and one with an aged clarinet of which he was consciously proud.

Gradually there crept over all who were present under the trees on that glorious day a sense of acute embarrassment. It was one of those long-drawn silences, in which people felt something had to be done; but what? Someone should make a request; but dared not. The children fidgeted. Could no one give a lead? But what; whither?

And then suddenly Nannie knew. She stood up, lifted her skirts, undid her suspenders, and peeling off her stockings, advanced with perfect dignity on the great tank. The fiddle and the clarinet broke into a vintage melody, the children shrieked with delight, the Greeks cheered and clapped, and the two younger diplomats were rolling up their trousers to join Nannie treading the grapes. Before many minutes his excellency and his lady were in the great vat too dancing with the rest as the music grew gradually faster and faster. At last a tired Nannie wine-red

Plate I. Attic red figure vase painting inside a Kylix painted by Epitetos,
c. 500 B.C. Boy with flutes and dancing girl with castanets.

Plate II. Attic red figure vase painting inside a Kylix painted by the
Gales painter, *c.* 500 B.C. Youth embracing flute-girl.

Plate III. Attic red figure vase painting outside a Kylix painted by the Foundry painter, c. 480 B.C. Naked flute-girl and revellers.

Plate IV. Attic red figure vase painting inside a Kylix painted by the Brygos painter, c. 470 B.C. Youth and dancing girl named Pilipos and Kalisto.

Plate V. Attic red figure vase painting on a hydria painted by Polygnotos, *c.* 440 B.C. Girls dancing and tumbling.

Plate VI. Attic red figure volute-Krater painted by the Pronomos painter, *c.* 410 B.C. Part of stage scene showing young Dionysos and Ariadne embracing.

Plate VII. "The Cup of Nestor." Gold, with double handles and two
doves perched by the rim, *c.* 1250 B.C.

Plate VIII (*a* and *b*). Part of the Hubbard Amphora, *c.* 900 B.C. A lady drinking wine from a syphon; on the left a Bull's Head Rhyton; and dancers on the other side.

Plate IX. Minoan Steatite Bull's Head Rhyton for pouring wine, *c.* 1450 B.C.
Height 7·1 ins. (the horns are modern).

Plate X. Shallow silver wine cup, diam. 8·8 inches, about 250 B.C. Inside in
high relief Dionysos and Ariadne kissing; a thyrsos between them.

Plate XI. Attic red figure vase from Camirus (early fourth century B.C.) with scene from a comedy

Plate XII. Attic red figure vase painting on the outside of a Kylix, painting by Makron, c. 490 B.C. Six Athenian Thyiads or Maenads. Another six are on the other side.

Plate XIII. Top of a bronze Kottabos-stand decorated with a
sphinx seated upon an Ionian capital. Perhaps Ionian work about
450–400 B.C.

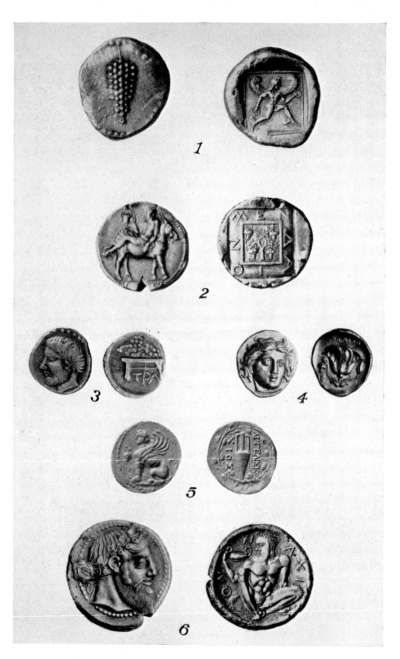

Plate XIV. Coins of various wine-producing states.
(1) Peparethos, silver, *c.* 500 B.C. Bunch of grapes and Eros. (2) Mende,
silver, *c.* 430 B.C. Dionysos on ass and small vine in a square. (3) Trapezus,
silver, *c.* 410 B.C. Male head and table loaded with grapes. (4) Rhodes,
gold, *c.* 400 B.C. Head of Helios and rose beside which bunch of grapes.
(5) Chios, copper, *c.* 200 B.C. Sphinx and pointed wine amphora. (6) Naxos
in Sicily, silver, *c.* 460 B.C. Head of Dionysos and squatting Seilenos with
wine cup.

Plate XV. Greek pottery wine amphora from Skiathos (1956) found in the sea, off Cape Artemision. Height 17 inches.

Plate XVI. The Corycian plain, 4000 feet above sea-level, looking east to the summit of Parnassus.

to above her knees and two children coloured to their waists, left
the wine-press, soon to be followed by the rest of the party.
What an omen of good all this was for Costa, who himself with
his friends and neighbours only went in to tread a measure after
his guests had opened the Ball.

❖❖❖❖❖❖❖❖❖❖❖❖❖❖❖❖❖❖ ❖❖❖❖❖❖❖❖❖❖❖❖❖❖❖❖❖❖

## Chapter Six

# BOTTLES,
# BEAKERS AND CUPS

❖❖❖❖❖❖❖❖❖❖❖❖❖❖❖❖❖❖❖❖❖❖❖❖❖❖❖❖❖❖❖❖❖❖❖❖

BY way of introduction to wine in the ancient world this little book opened with the description of a Symposium in fifth-century Athens, a wine party, vividly described by Xenophon. Now that the subject is to be the shapes and uses of containers and cups employed for wine, a return to Athens is called for since it is there that we may get the best of impressions by a review of the "vases" made by Athenians in the sixth, fifth and fourth centuries B.C. Potters, of course, produced many an object which was in no way connected with wine: scent-bottles and soap-bottles, ointment bottles and oil-jars, spools and dice-boxes, plates and powder-jars, lamps, oil-fillers and great prize vases for victors in the games. Nevertheless, a majority of their splendid products were made for the complex ceremonials of drinking at the banquets of aristocrats, or for the simple use of less opulent wine lovers. And many of the finer pieces were exported to regions far from Athens because these works of art—for such they were—found a market in remote regions like the Crimea, Philistia, Libya and the Sudan, in countless western and northern Greek colonies, among the opulent Etruscans, and even among Germanic chieftains on the upper Rhine.

They make a special appeal to our imagination because they played an active part in the life of the Greeks. Though they now rest quietly on the shelves of museum cases, they once led a busy existence. They were taken to and from the fountains, filled and refilled at banquets, carried about by athletes, used by women during their toilet, and brought as gifts to brides; they performed a rôle in religious ceremonies, were taken by mourners to graves, and sent in ships to distant lands.[1]

Other Greek industrial states produced plentiful vases of their own, especially common unpainted household ware. Corinth, however, and Sparta, Chios and Clazomenae, Rhodes and Delos, turned out, at one time or another, painted vases with enchanting decoration and lively figures and scenes upon them. Western potters made vases called "Chalcidian", "Caeretan" and "Pontic", the sources of Etruscan imitation of Greek ceramics. All these are much rarer than Athenian wares and therefore often more desired by those museums and collectors who continue to acquire vases. In earlier chapters we have had occasion to mention, describe, and illustrate, vases used for wine in earlier civilisations. Steatite bull's-head firkins (Pl. IX), gold and silver goblets, a cup like the Homeric cup of Nestor (Pl. VII), have been described. A great eighth-century bowl from Cyprus decorated with a variety of vases for wine has been shown (Pl. VIII). But for the highest artistic merit there are none that can compete with the best products of Athens for that feeling for rhythm and structure and shape which the ancient Greeks possessed to so high a degree, and which showed itself in the work of every gifted artist. The magic of the Parthenon, of the bronze Zeus from Artemisium, of a young marble girl in a simple *peplos*, of a bronze horse or helmet reappears in perfectly designed and shaped Athenian vases.

Compared with the vases of other countries, which are designed mostly in continuous curves, Greek pottery is strongly articulated. The various parts—mouth, neck, body, foot—are generally set off from one another, lip and foot are often in several degrees, and handles are usually added. . . . In the shapes the influence of contemporary

[1] G. M. A. Richter and M. J. Milne, *Shapes and Names of Athenian Vases*, p. xiv.

metalware can often be detected; and sometimes even such details as handle attachments and heads of rivets are copied in clay. But always the difference of material is taken into account and the precise metal shapes are translated into rounded, plastic forms.[2]

And the vases are well adapted to their various uses. Wine jugs have round or trefoil-shaped mouths, constructed so that the wine can be poured out without spilling, and unexpectedly the remarkable shape of a vessel like the wide open kylix (Figs. 8 and 9), that has been compared to a modern champagne glass, is perfectly designed as a drinking cup, because the slight convex curve on the inside of the rim prevents wine from running down both cheeks when a reveller leans his head backward so as to drain the dregs. The great kraters (Figs. 10, 11, 12, 13), or mixing bowls, are always wide-mouthed and therefore perfectly designed either for having liquid poured into them or for having liquids taken out with ladles. Hydriae, or water jars (Fig. 14) have fairly narrow

Fig. 8. Stemmed Kylix.

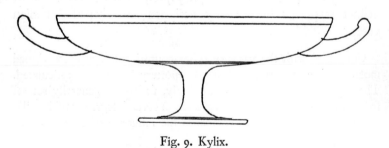

Fig. 9. Kylix.

[2] *Op. cit.*, p. xi.

Fig. 10. Krater (Column-krater).

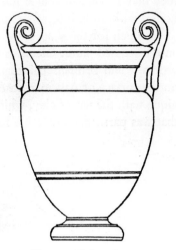

Fig. 11. Volute-krater.

Fig. 12. Krater (Bell-krater).

Fig. 13. Kalyx-krater.

necks and heavy feet, and they are functional vases built so that they may be carried almost full from the outdoor fountain to the house, without letting water spill over.

So much for the shapes, the details of which will be described and discussed later. Meanwhile one may consider the extraordinary and brilliant painting and decoration which appeared on the surface of Athenian vases. Potters had built up their technique with the use of clay, which, when fired, produced a surface that was particularly suitable for drawing and painting.

Fig. 14. Hydria.

Nowadays when your artist makes a sketch he naturally takes the handy, inexpensive sheet of paper on which to draw. The Greek had no paper. He had papyrus, but that was an expensive import from Egypt, reserved for the serious things of life—books, poems, legal documents, business receipts and contracts. No artist could easily afford papyrus, and he would have found the surface rather too rough-grained if he could. School children worked on wooden slates coated with wax; and the ordinary man wishing to make a brief note or to cast his vote by ballot in the assembly stretched out his hand not for a pencil and a scrap of paper, but for a nail and a pot-sherd. The inscribed *ostraka*, or sherds, found in Athens bearing the names of politicians destined for ostracism, were the scribbling-paper of the ancient Athenian; the complete vase was the drawing-paper of the Attic artist—the cheapest base for the exercise of his art. Therefore, let it not be thought that Attic vase-painters can be roughly equated with the worthy craftsmen who decorated Crown Derby or Delft, Majolica or Meissen china, or with those who added tedious painting to the lifeless pottery of Sèvres. Some mere craftsmen made drawings on cheap, mass-production Attic wares, of course; but, in addition to these, brilliant draughtsmen of the first rank wandered from pottery to pottery and drew master-pieces of design on cups and pots.

Contemplating Athenian vases of the highest quality one is driven to speculate a little; for one asks, why was so much trouble taken to decorate something so fragile with pictures of such excellence? And then one tries to find an explanation. Evidence abounds to show that the ancient Greeks had a sensibility greater than any people before them or after them for the fine arts in their most subtle guise. But, if that be admitted, we have still not answered the question "Why do these paintings on pots?" Numerous archaeologists would explain the phenomenon as follows. In the sixth, fifth and fourth centuries B.C. it had occurred to no one to decorate with frescoes or other types of paintings the inside walls of private houses. Apparently, too, no one had thought to produce panel paintings for hanging on the walls. In fact, the man who could afford such luxuries would acquire a vase suitable for exhibition on the "sideboard" and for practical use as well when he gave a symposium or party. Evidence of his good taste might have appeared in the selection of his painted pottery and in possessing pots that were fairly frequently signed by well-known potters and painters of his day. There exists a great Athenian mixing bowl in Florence, produced about 560 B.C., carrying two signatures which, translated, read: "Ergotimos made it", "Kleitias painted it". Obviously value was attached to the signatures of the artists who made such things. Therefore it seems permissible to imagine that an Athenian—call him Glaukon—visiting his friend Myron, walks over to the "sideboard", takes a look at the vases and, turning to Myron, remarks, "I see you have just bought a new Exekias"—just, almost, as a modern might say, "I see you have acquired a new Picasso."

Wine vases were of two distinct classes: those made for the preparation of the drink, and those from which people drank. Pots and cups—the classification is simple. Pots were of three types: the wine jar, the water-jug and the open mixing-bowl; in Greek amphora, hydria and krater. Cups were also of three main types, the wide-open, stemmed vase for light drinks, the deep vase with a foot and two upswept handles and the deep bowl for heavy wine—in Greek, kylix, kantharos and kotyle!

*Amphora:* a vase with a more or less oval body, a low foot, a wide mouth and two vertical handles; the principal varieties of shape are known as *Tyrrhenian, Panathenaic* (Fig. 15), *Panel* (Fig. 16), *Neck* and *Nolan* (Fig. 17) *amphorae:* used principally for wine, but also for corn, honey, oil and other commodities.

*Hydria:* a vase with an oval body which is joined by a fairly flat shoulder to the neck; it has three handles; two horizontal for carrying the vase when full and one vertical, generally rising above the level of the lip, for carrying when empty; used for water (Fig. 14).

*Krater:* a large two-handled bowl, varying in shape, used for the mixing of wine and water; the principal shapes are: the *Bell-krater* (Fig. 12), resembling an inverted bell, the lip projecting above the body, the handles attached horizontally to the sides: the *Column-krater* (Fig. 10), wide-bellied, with a short, wide neck, a flat rim joined to the shoulder by solid columnar handles; the *Kalyx-krater* (Fig. 13), resembling the opening calyx of a flower, the lip projecting above the body, the handles attached to the lower part of the body; the *Volute-krater* (Fig. 11), with an oval body, large neck and lip, large handles reaching above the lip and curved round in volutes.

So much for the big pots; and now for cups:

Fig. 15. Amphora.                Fig. 16. Amphora.

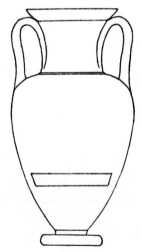

Fig. 17. Nolan Amphora.

*Kylix:* a drinking cup with a stem, high at first (Fig. 8), but tending to grow shorter as the bowl of the cup grows shallower (Fig. 9), two handles attached horizontally to the sides; the *Eye-kylix* is an archaic form with pairs of eyes painted on each side; used for wine.

*Kantharos:* a cup with a deep bowl and a stem, two loop-shaped vertical handles rising above the rim, attached to the rim and to the lower edge of the body; used for wine (Fig. 18).

*Kotyle:* a bowl-shaped cup with a flat foot, slightly curved sides, and two flat handles level with the rim; used for wine (Fig. 19). A kind of beaker.

Fig. 18. Kantharos.          Fig. 19. Kotyle.

Two more utensils call for mention in order to complete the picture: the ladle and the wine-jug: *kyathos* and *oinochoe.*

*Kyathos:* a ladle in the form of a cup with a foot and a long upswept handle; it can be dipped into the wine without wetting the finger. However, many of these utensils were of metal, in which case they were like very long-handled soup or gravy spoons.

*Oinochoe:* a jug often with trefoil lip. Numerous and varied shapes occur, some with upswept handles so that the jug could be dipped. Its origin is early, for *oinochoai* in a row are shown on the famous painted mixing-bowl from Cyprus (Pl. VIII).

And now the ceremony of mixing and serving, which actually goes back to Homeric times, may be described. Girls of the household have been to the nearest well-house and brought back *hydriai* filled with cold spring water. Meanwhile a man-servant has been to the cellar to bring up a large rough pointed *amphora* from the store. The wine from this is next decanted into one or two handsome painted *amphorai*, and with the aid of a *kyathos* so many measures of wine and so many measures of water are ladled into the great *krater* which stands ready. Sometimes, though, the wine, before mixing, might be poured into a special type of vase serving as a wine-cooler which was stood in a very large *krater*, and which had snow packed round it. High among the summits of mount Parnes to the north of Athens there is often snow to be found in hollow patches such as the sun never touches, and snow could be packed into skins and brought down in the cool of a morning on the backs of animals. Some years ago on my way up Parnes in May, I met a man carrying a dripping sack of snow, which he said he was taking down to his village in the plain for his little daughter who was ill with a fever.

It is always a matter of surprise to learn how constantly the ancient Greeks mixed water with their wine. According to a late authority a favourite proportion was one part of wine to three parts of water. This raises the reflection that some wine must have been very strong indeed, having a "proof" that can perhaps now be paralleled in the heavy, heady red wine of Paros and of Santorini—potent stuff. Light wines and the good medicinal *retinites* would assuredly be taken unwatered. The wine served us at a Greek symposium might probably taste odd at first; but we should, no doubt, acquire the taste, as many of us have acquired a taste for *retsina*. The difficulty would rather be the unknown spirituous content. A Greek would not have phrased it thus, unfamiliar as he was with chemical alcohol. But he reacted, as we do, to intoxicating drink; and this was usually his reason for diluting wine at feasts. In Plato's *Symposium*, when talk has gone on all through the night, Socrates rises from his place with the dawn and leaves in Aristodemus' company, both of them sober. Perhaps one may hazard the guess that it was the predictable strength—the "proof"—of the famous brands from Mende,

Lesbos, Chios or Rhodes, rather than their estimation in terms of vintages and "years", that caused their popularity. As with the proprietary brands of Scotch whisky today, you did know what you were getting. But poor wine, unfamiliar wine—like hard cider from the wood, drunk at some small West-country farm—could bring disaster, as we may learn from what is perhaps the funniest drinking story in ancient literature. A famous historian of the fourth century B.C., Timaeus of Tauromenium in Sicily, told of what happened to a party of young men who had come by sea to Akragas (Agrigento) from some other part of the Greek world. His tale runs as follows:

In Akragas there is a house which is called the "trireme" from the following circumstances. A party of young men were drinking in it, and became so wild when over-heated by the liquor, that they imagined they were sailing in a trireme, and that they were in a bad storm on the seas. Finally they completely lost their senses, and tossed all the furniture and bedding out of the house as though upon the waters convinced that the captain directed them to lighten ship because of the raging storm. Well, a great crowd gathered and began to carry off the jetsam, but even then the young men did not cease from their mad actions. Next day police appeared at the house and lodged a complaint against the young men when they were still half-seas over. Questioned by the Magistrates, they answered that they had been much put to it by the storm and had been compelled to throw into the sea the super-fluous cargo. When the authorities expressed surprise at their insanity, one of the young men, though he appeared to be the oldest of the company, said to them, "Noble Tritons, I was so frightened that I threw myself into the lowest possible place in the hold and lay there." The Magistrates, therefore, pardoned their delirium, but warned them never to drink too much and let them go, and they gratefully promised (to be careful). "If", said the oldest, "we make port after this awful tempest, we shall raise altars in our country to you as Saviours Manifest, side by side with the Sea Gods, because you appeared to us so opportunely." That is why the house was called the "trireme".

The fascination of the painting on Athenian vases is enhanced by the infinite variety of the subjects depicted upon them.[3]

3 See the Bibliography at the end of this book.

Again the division into the pots and cups aids us to a brief account of the subjects, and we begin with the pots. These provide comparatively large surfaces and many have panels—one on either side—for pictures. At first vases of all kinds were "black-figure", the subject drawn and painted in black, with added red and white, on the terracotta body of pot or cup. "Red-figure", invented about 530 B.C., began very gradually to displace the older "black-figure" though the two co-existed for nearly fifty years.

Big vases, the pots, were decorated most frequently with religious and mythological subjects: the Gods, Herakles and his exploits, Homeric heroes in combat, the departure of heroes for the wars, Theseus and his Acts, and constantly—because the pots were to serve for wine—the wine-god himself, Dionysos, accompanied by Maenads and Seilenos. But outdoor and domestic scenes were not wanting: soldiers, athletes and other youths, musicians, spinners and weavers, and naked bathing girls.

Cups at first carried religious and mythological scenes like some of the big pots, but on a smaller scale. At one stage their rims were decorated with single miniature figures of the utmost daintiness. Generally painting a cup involved a designing and spacing and drawing very different from the painting of a pot; and artists tended to specialise either in the one or the other, although a few of them painted on both kinds of vases. A cup, especially a wide open cup like a *kylix*, afforded space for three pictures, one on each side upon the cup's outside, and a fine circular "tondo" inside the very middle of the cup. Because these vessels were made for the sole purpose of drinking wine there were two subjects shown with increasing frequency; the one religious and orgiastic, the other secular and gay—*thiasos* and *komos*—the former bacchic revel and rout, the latter carousal and merry-making.

With themes such as these the inside picture was often related to the continuous frieze of maenads and selenoi with Dionysos on the outside of the cup, and the cup's "tondo" might depict the god himself, or a maenad of haunting beauty, god-possessed. And *komos* pictures could supply an amusing counterpart; for the outside of the cup might show revellers reclining, dancing, singing to the music of naked flute-girls, and boy lyre-players (Pls. I–IV), while within the cup a picture awaited the merry-maker as he drained his wine, a picture that might be something of a surprise. One *kylix* contains a useful warning against the excess of drunkenness. An elegant youth, standing up, is in distress, he is being very sick and vomiting on the floor while a kind and charming little short-haired slave-girl holds the poor young man's head for him. On occasion there appeared a subject which our peculiar civilisation forbids us to illustrate, driving certain Athenian cups into the dark arcana of Museum cupboards, the subject—elegantly and passionately rendered—of coitus between a reveller and a *hetaira*, or girl-friend.4 As the guest at a Greek symposium slowly drained the cup of dark wine which had been given to him he must have gazed with no lack of pleasure at the little painting inside. Some cups were made of metal, especially silver, in the fourth and later centuries. A delicate silver phiale, like a stemless kylix, one of a pair found at Tarentum (Pl. X) about 250 B.C. shows, inside, Dionysos and Ariadne kissing, the top of a thyrsos between them.

4 Before missionaries imposed their sour codes in the Pacific such public demonstrations of sexual intercourse were frequent among the beautiful and uninhibited young people of Polynesia even down to the last century. See Bengt Danielsson, *Love in the South Seas*, London, 1954, *passim*.

*Chapter Seven*

❖❖❖❖❖❖❖❖❖❖❖❖❖❖❖❖❖❖❖❖❖❖❖❖❖❖❖❖❖❖❖❖❖❖❖❖❖❖❖

# WINE, WOMEN . . .

❖❖❖❖❖❖❖❖❖❖❖❖❖❖❖❖❖❖❖❖❖❖❖❖❖❖❖❖❖❖❖❖❖❖❖❖❖❖❖

WOMEN in the ancient Greek world were—as I have en-
deavoured to point out elsewhere[1]—a fortunate and well-
balanced lot of creatures as contrasted with their despised and
down-trodden great-granddaughterly descendants of the dark
and Middle Ages. Those fortunate conditions applied to the
respectable wives and daughters of Athenians as they did to their
carefree sisters in Sparta and Ionia. Men who still cling to the out-
worn belief that Athenian women lived almost in "purdah"
become scarcer as time goes on. There is wishful thinking present
because some men—regarding fifth-century Athens as the home
of perfection while they are themselves of misogynist bent—
want to believe in the insignificance of Athenian women. All very
nonsensical—as has several times been shown.[2]

Far be it from me, however, to deny that the "respectable"
women of Athens had a tendency to drink too much. This did not
apply to the *hetairai,* the girl-friends who often took part in the
men's symposia, because they drank wine carefully mixed with
water in accordance with the rules described in the last chapter.
They were precise and masculine rules, for in general men are
planners. But women have been, since the very beginnings of
organised communal life, improvisors, and this is apparent even

[1] Seltman, *Women in Antiquity* (Pan Books, 1956) enlarged edition
(Thames and Hudson, 1956).
[2] Seltman, *op. cit.*; H. D. F. Kitto, *The Greeks*, pp. 219 ff.

95

today in a number of professions calling for precision and planning.[3] Once a man becomes interested in the art of cooking food, he usually turns out to be a better chef than a woman, only because he measures with accuracy his ounces and his teaspoons where she guesses and approximates. She gets results, original and interesting, but she is rarely able to serve exactly the same dish twice. This is, of course, by no means an infallible rule; only a useful generalisation. The point is that a woman who will hazard a guess in the kitchen will also hazard a guess in the buttery if she is preparing wine; and in ancient Athens she probably put less water with it than her husband would have done; often, indeed, she preferred to take her wine neat; and, as has been shown, neat wine was often very potent. Therefore it was the respectable wives—rather than the gay girl-friends—who were inclined to overdo potations, and some of them, naturally, showed intoxication more than did others.

Observation proves that the reactions of individuals—whether male or female—to wine is very varied indeed. At one end I have observed a young woman grow merry and slightly irresponsible on a single glass of sherry; and at the other end a charming young person who needed the better part of two bottles of vintage claret to release the sparkle of her wit.

Tippling among Athenian women probably increased in the second half of the fifth century B.C., when too many of the men were away at the wars too often. In the absence of the master more responsibility falls almost inevitably upon the mistress of the household. Whether it be Agamemnon off to the Siege of Troy, or a Spartiate going to invest Messene, or an Athenian hoplite headed for Sicily and disaster, or Alexander riding to conquer the dusty and glittering East, the fact is clear that Clytaemnestra and Gorgo and Lysistrata and Olympias gain immensely in power. And though the gallant soldier may ponder on the possibility of an ardent wife taking the occasional lover, he will still feel his affairs to be safer in the hands of his spouse that in those of uncle, brother, nephew, or even son.

3 Seltman, *op. cit.*, Chapter I.

Though the principle is general, it is not, of course, universal in application. Yet one may observe that it took the First World War to give women the vote in Britain, and the second to enfranchise the women of France, while in contrast that most democratic of free countries, Switzerland, unscathed by war for so many generations, is almost alone in refusing the vote to its female half.4

Anyhow the three surviving plays by Aristophanes about women are certain evidence of their increasing influence—wantonness many Athenian men would have called it—in Athenian society. They began more and more to do what they liked, and drinking wine was one of the things they did like. We must be prepared to accept the general themes of Aristophanes' three "women plays" as factual evidence—not for feminism among Athenian men—but for a state of affairs which, in Athenian society, was getting out of hand. These comedies were only funny because the theme of each one of them was rather too "near the bone", and because a poet, of such genius as Aristophanes possessed, knew that one way of ameliorating a gnawing worry was to bring it out and caricature it. Even today the hen-pecked little husband will enjoy a farce depicting a suspicious wife-bully so that he can say to himself, "Well, my old woman's not quite as bad as that!" Carefree bachelors and contented spouses are not amused.

The play which most emphasises the wine-bibbing of Athenian fifth-century women was the *Thesmophoriazusae* of 411 B.C.

"Festival Women" might serve as an English title for this play, produced in the very same year as *Lysistrata*, but later. There was an annual three-day festival, for women only, held in honour of Demeter Thesmophoros, goddess of corn and ordered life. That is the setting for the comedy which is a fierce attack on the dramatist Euripides for anti-feminism shown in his plays. When the play opens we learn that the women of Athens have planned to punish Euripides for insults and they are about to discuss his case at their meeting in the Thesmophorion. He

4 *Op. cit.*, pp. 141 f.

believes that they will condemn him to death unless someone
attends the meeting to defend him. Therefore he and his father-
in-law, Mnesilochus, visit Agathon in Queer Street, begging him
to impersonate a woman and speak in Euripides' favour. On his
refusal, the father-in-law agrees to take on the job, is shaved, has
his body-hair removed, and is dressed up in female garments.
Next the scene shifts to the Thesmophorion, and the debate on
Euripides begins. The fun soon develops into a riot when the
women are informed that there is a man in their midst. Mnesilochus, the false female, is suspected, challenged; had she ever
been to this Festival before?

Yes.

Well, what did we do first?

We drank.

That answer passes, but they insist on a personal inspection
and discover A MAN!

The situation grows desperate and the police are coming; but
before they arrive Mnesilochus is likely to be torn in pieces by
the furious women. One of them, Mika, holds in her arms her
baby girl wrapped in a saffron robe. Mnesilochus in a panic
snatches her child from her to use it as a hostage and clings to the
altar of Dionysos on which lies a sacrificial knife beside a sacred
cup. It is now that a farcical dialogue ensues, bubbling with mock-
tragedy.

MIKA: Where is he flying to? Stop him! stop him! Ah! miserable me!
he has torn my child from my breast and has disappeared with it.

MNESILOCHUS: Scream as loud as you like, but it'll never suck your
bosom again. If you don't let me go this very instant I shall slit the
veins of its thighs with this knife and its blood will flow over the altar.

MIKA: Oh! great gods! oh! friends, help me! terrify him with your
shrieks, attack this monster, don't let him rob me of my only child.

CHORUS: Oh! oh! venerable Parcae, what fresh attack is this? 'Tis
the crowning act of audacity and shamelessness! What has he done
now, friends, what has he done?

MNESILOCHUS: Ah! this insolence passes all bounds, but I shall know
how to curb it.

98

CHORUS: What a shameful deed! the measure of his iniquities is full!

MIKA: Aye, it's shameful that he should have robbed me of my child.

CHORUS: 'Tis past belief to be so criminal and so impudent!

MNESILOCHUS: Ah! you're not near the end of it yet.

MIKA: Little I care whence you come; you shall never return to boast of having acted so odiously with impunity. You shall be punished.

MNESILOCHUS: You won't do it, by the gods!

CHORUS: And what immortal would protect you for your crime?

*The Chorus closes in on him at the altar*

MNESILOCHUS: You talk in vain; I shall not let the child go.

CHORUS: By the goddesses, you will not laugh presently over your crime and your impious speech. For with impiety, as 'tis meet, shall we reply to your impiety. Soon fortune will turn round and overwhelm you. Come! bring wood along. Let us burn the wretch, let us roast him as quickly as possible.

MIKA: (*to her serving maid*) Bring faggots, Mania! (*To Mnesilochus*) You will be mere charcoal soon.

MNESILOCHUS: Grill away, roast me! (*He looks at the child and pulls its robe off*) But you, my child, take off this Cretan robe and blame no one but your mother for your death. But what ever is this! The little girl is nothing but a skin filled with wine and shod with Persian slippers. Oh! you wanton, you tippling women, who think of nothing but wine; you are a fortune to the drinking-shops and are our ruin; for the sake of drink, you neglect both your household and your shuttles!

MIKA: (*to her maid*) Faggots, Mania, plenty of them.

MNESILOCHUS: Bring as many as you like. But answer me; are you the mother of this brat?

MIKA: I carried it nine months.

MNESILOCHUS: You carried it?

MIKA: I swear it by Artemis.

MNESILOCHUS: How much does it hold? Three pints? Tell me.

MIKA: Oh! what have you done? You have stripped the poor child quite naked, and it is so small, so small.

MNESILOCHUS: So small?

MIKA: Yes, quite small to be sure.

99

MNESILOCHUS: How old is it? Has it seen the Feast of Cups three or four times?

MIKA: It was born about the time of the last Dionysia. But give it back to me.

MNESILOCHUS: No, may Apollo bear me witness!

MIKA: (*to the other women*) Well, then we are going to burn him.

MNESILOCHUS: Burn me, but then I shall rip this open instantly.

MIKA: No, no, I adjure you, don't; do anything you like to me rather than that.

MNESILOCHUS: What a tender mother you are; but nevertheless I shall rip it open. (*Cuts open the wine skin*)

MIKA: Oh, my beloved daughter! Mania, quick the sacred cup, so that I may at least catch the blood of my child.

MNESILOCHUS: Hold it below; it is the sole favour I grant you.

MIKA: Curse you, you pitiless monster! (*She drains the sacred cup of Dionysos*)

Next there comes a Choral interlude and the Leader delivers a speech in which the virtues of men and women are compared, greatly to the advantage of the latter. A constable arrives and Mnesilochus is kept under arrest in the charge of a Scythian policeman, and Euripides, like a quick-change artist, appears in a variety of disguises in the hope of persuading the policeman to let the old man go. His last ruse succeeds when he appears dressed up as an elderly Madame accompanied by two little strumpets who lure the policeman away, and father-in-law escapes.

It has been said that this is perhaps the best comedy of them all. "Nowhere else do we find so perfect a blend of animal and intellectual ingredients embodied in a play so skilfully constructed and so artistically unified."[5]

On an Attic red figure hydria (Pl. XI) now in the British Museum and dated to about 380 B.C. there is shown an abbreviated version of this rollicking comedy. Dionysos, left, is horrified because the supposed child is to be sacrificed at his altar; on the right the Scythian policeman is likewise shocked; in the centre is Mnesilochus somewhat ineffectively disguised as a woman,

5 Seltman, *Women in Antiquity* (Pan Books edition), p. 117.

knife in his right hand, and, on his left arm the "little-girl wine-skin", hair hanging down but without a face.[6]

If emphasis has so far been placed on the particular inclination of Athenian women for wine-drinking, that is because we know so much more about them than about their sisters in other Greek States. Monuments are of no great help since a drunken woman is even more unaesthetic than a drunken man, and therefore rarely, if ever, depicted in Greek art. There does exist a marble statue in Munich of an old inebriate hag hugging a wine amphora, her head rolling and her toothless mouth agape.[7] The figure was attributed by Pliny to a Boeotian sculptor called Myron who had settled at Smyrna in Ionia in the second century B.C. This statue is, however, something of a generalisation of the fact that old women sometimes get drunk and not necessarily an indictment of Ionian habits. The goings-on of women in Italy will be mentioned in a later chapter.

Accordingly we may at this point return to study the drinking habits of Athenian women with special reference to one of their most important and most remarkable religious practices—the pilgrimage to Delphi of the Thyiads, those mystic, god-possessed women of Athens.

People who of a sudden impulse abandon the social routine, the looms and shuttles, of their group, deserting parents, spouses or children in order to indulge any form of private, personal, emotionally religious practice, are certain to incur resentment, for they are being all too literally "un-popular". Periodic bouts of Dionysiac frenzy may have come to Greek villages and tiny townships in the seventh century B.C. and caused not only resentment but even some persecution of the cult by conventional persons. By the beginning of the sixth century, however, some cities of Greece were growing fairly large, and for such Bacchos Bromios, with his mysteries that drove the women wildly to the mountains, became a subject of the very gravest concern.

[6] For a different explanation (wrong, I think) see A. B. Cook, *Zeus*, i, pp. 654 f.

[7] A. W. Lawrence, *Classical Sculpture*, p. 299; Pl. 108b.

It has already been suggested,[8] that it was the Thracian wine-god Bacchos Bromios who became identified, after the customary Greek fashion, with an older god of wine and corn—a minor god, known to Homer—whose name, Dionysos, is found on one of the early Mycenaean tablets. What happened when the authorities tried to ban or repress this wild cult is, as we have seen, the theme of the *Bacchae* of Euripides. Fortunately for the Greeks there were few to take the line which Pentheus took. There are indications that the whole trouble was resolved during the first half of the sixth century B.C. by the actions of three brilliant Greek statesmen, and in characteristic Greek fashion. In important centres the cult of Dionysos was taken into the mechanism of the state cults. Periander, who ruled in Corinth from about 625 to 585 B.C., deliberately introduced a Dionysiac festival into the richest Greek city of the day. His neighbour Cleisthenes, Despot of Sicyon, displaced the cult of an old local hero by the cult of Dionysos. Moreover, Cleisthenes, who, supporting the Delphians in a local war with Crisa and commanding the allied forces, founded the quadrennial Pythian Games in 582 B.C. at Delphi, may have been the man who introduced the actual worship of Dionysos into Delphi. Or, if he did not bring it in, he so strengthened and encouraged it as to give to Bacchos a status only second to that of Pythian Apollo. The Holy Sepulchre of Dionysos was placed in the secret underground *adyton* of the temple beside the navel-stone of "Earth" and the sacred Tripod of the Pythia. Thus to combine the realms of the careful god of law and order, and of the mystical god of licence and abandon, was one of the most startling examples of Greek genius for adjustment. Law could be redeemed from mechanistic rote by the human natural contact of the anarchic god, while licence could be put under control by coupling it with the god of self-knowledge and moderation. Order should learn about disorder, and disorder about order.

Corinth, Sicyon, Delphi were three places, Athens being the fourth, where great skill was used to accommodate the Dionysiac

[8] See pp. 50 f., 62, above.

trouble. Peisistratus ruled Athens from 566 B.C.; and, at about
the time when he founded the Panathenaic games for Athene,
he also instituted the Great Dionysia. That is to say, he brought
into Athens and installed at the foot of the Acropolis, the ancient
wooden statue of Dionysos from Attic Eleutherae, on the frontier
of Boeotia, a village which was claiming to be the god's birth-
place. With the statue came its priest and his little company of
village mummers called "goat-singers"—in Greek *tragōdoi*—
country lads and devotees of the god who at times kept company
with the local village "maenads", the god-possessed girls who
wandered in the woods of mount Cithaeron. Then Athenian
vase-painters began to picture the god travelling on an ass or a
ship, or in a winged car (Fig. 20).

Of a sudden the whole thing assumed a new importance. Very
early performances took place in the *orchēstra*, or dancing place,

Fig. 20. Dionysos holding Kantharos and grapes seated on winged car
preceded by Seilenos carrying vases.

in the Athenian agora on the north side of the Acropolis; the spectators sitting on wooden benches so unsafe that they once collapsed. For this reason the theatre was transferred to the south side of the Acropolis close to the little archaic temple of Dionysos. Many people hold that this shift took place as early as the sixth century B.C.9 Anyhow, a primitive type of play-acting, which had gone on in the god's village home, suddenly turned into something very different. The original professional author-actor was Thespis, who won a prize for tragedy in 534 B.C. and was the first to appear as an actor separate from the Chorus, speaking set speeches, changing his rôle as he changed masks, and playing several parts within a play. Structures like tents or booths served as dressing-rooms, but it is not known what background may have been arranged behind the shallow platform or stage. From this, the first state-sponsored theatre, Attic drama and Greek drama in general continued to develop along its own impressive lines.

It was a small beginning when they ranged some wooden seats for spectators in a semi-circle, and put up a little stage on to which the first mummer leapt to tell his tale, while the others answered back and sang short choruses. Here the *tragōdoi* created for a city audience "tragedy", and the theatre was born. Presently "revel-singers"—*kōmōdoi*—produced shows of another kind and "comedy" came into being. Yet it was all built round the cult of Dionysos; and it canalised a great flood of energy that would otherwise have found anarchical outlets elsewhere. It did this for the men. But not for the women. In their case Delphi had to help.

"Thyiads" was the name used both in Athens and at Delphi—but not, apparently, elsewhere—for "Maenads", the women in *ecstasis*; and this formed so strong a link between the women and girls of both communities that they established a joint biennial enterprise for the impelling mysteries. No certain date can be given for the beginning of this union of Thyiads from two places so far apart from one another; but it may well have been started

9 See Ida Thallon Hill, *The Ancient City of Athens*, p. 114.

after the days of Peisistratus and at the time when the Athenian Alcmaeonid family were in control of Athens. That would be towards the end of the sixth century B.C. Late in the summer or autumn of every second year the Chief Priest of Athens selected a troupe of women and girls from among the best Athenian families to be Thyiads for the State. No certainty exists about their number but, as figures, fourteen and sixteen have been suggested; and it is not likely that there were more than a score of them in any year. A fine Attic vase painted about 490 B.C. depicts a dozen of them (Pl. XII). There was doubtless a woman experienced, but like Lysistrata relatively young and active, who had made the expedition several times and was therefore the Leader. At Delphi such a one was "Principal"—at least in later days; and Plutarch, when priest at Delphi, valued the Senior Thyiad, Klea, as an intimate friend. But the Athenian women and girls chosen to be Thyiads were committed to weeks of hard outdoor life; for, starting in late October, they had to make their way on foot from Athens, by way of Eleusis, Eleutherae, Plataea, Thebes, Lebadeia, Panopeus and Arachova, to Delphi. It was a route little short of a hundred miles, traversing rough, steep mountain-passes; and it may be reckoned today as about forty-five walking hours, or five walking days. There were, of course, rests on the pilgrimage; they stopped in towns where Dionysos was worshipped to perform their dances, as Pausanias, the traveller, learnt from personal conversation with some Thyiads as late as the second century of our era. No need, of course, to take wine with them for wherever these "holy women" rested they could have all they required. Perhaps they were ten days or more on the way. Yet such a walk undertaken barefoot in early winter proves that the young women and girls of Athens were assuredly tough. The once popular notion that Athenian females were dull, unenterprising creatures, as physically inadequate as though they had never stepped outside of a convent or a seraglio, and therefore held in disdain by the men, is now ceasing to be maintained with conviction. The Thyiads are one more example, if such be needed, of some temporary independence and of audacious activity on the women's part.

It is November and the news has come that the Athenians are near. The Delphian girls go out to meet them. An hour's journey away the two throngs mingle happily. Together they pass below the crag of Hyampia, from which the great rocks had crashed down upon the greedy Medes. Together they enter the precinct gate and wind up the paved way past the east front of Apollo's temple and along its north side to that place which is the "temple" of Dionysos—the theatre. Every theatre is a temple of Bromios; and the subconscious knowledge of its ineluctable consecration to the spirit of the god may explain why even to our own day "ciphers to this great accompt on your imaginary forces work". The Delphic theatre, up at the highest corner of the Sacred Precinct, was at first a semi-circular hollow scooped from the mountain-side and only later built of solid stone. From this the Thyiads pass into the township of Delphi to stay with their hosts, whom one may assume to have been Thyiads too, or the parents of Thyiad girls. If you have been to the place early in the winter season, you can more easily picture the setting and the view. To the south and west the sea in the gulf of Itea looks oddly like quicksilver, and the mountains, half-veiled in cloud, seem very distant. From the gorge of the river Pleistos below, with its long dark green mat of olive trees joining the huge olive-tree carpet of the Itean plain, mists lift and gather and build themselves into clouds, which rise still higher as though hurrying to join the towering mass that shrouds Parnassus. When the sun comes fitfully through, he still gives warmth, but the shadows have a wintry chill. In that setting and climate, imagination may picture what happens after a few days of rest for the Athenians. At sunset the air is tense with a knowledge that Mystery is soon to begin. The Thyiads are gathered in the theatre's circular orchestra, fawn-skins falling over their pleated robes. Each holds a thyrsos; some have castanets or little drums; some hold young animals in their arms. The evening draws in, and a few Bacchoi climb up the steps holding lighted torches; someone touches a drum and a sigh goes up. At the altar in the centre the priest of Dionysos cuts the throat of a young he-goat, a sacrifice to Bromios who is coming to possess his votaries. Bacchos is not merely the wine-god but the god of all natural fluids—wine and honey, milk and such others as betoken a god of fertility. The blood of the goat runs out on to the altar, down on to the pavement. Strange that either fasting *or* raw meat, scourge *or* thyrsos, the tolled bell *or* the beaten drum, the body buried in the hooded habit *or* naked limbs dancing upon the mountain top, may equally produce a sense of mystical union with God.

High up on the Bad Stair[10] a shepherd youth, with a tail of horsehair tied on to make one think him a satyr, puts his double flutes to his lips. The thin weird notes are magnified and repeated by echoes. A girl in the theatre screams and flings back her head. "Euohi, euohi, He comes!" Drum, and another drum; rhythm and the castanets begin to clapper. It has grown almost dark, for the torches seem brighter now. They are moving up through the gangways between the rows of seats and out to the highest corner where the path leads straight to the Bad Stair. The whole throng of Thyiads follows the torch-bearers for "Bromios leads his revellers to the mountains, to the mountains". You, the barbarian from another land, may sit there alone in the theatre, wrapped in your warmest cloak, and look up to the mountain-side to see the torch-lights slowly rising in zigzags up that wild track, while snatches of the music of Bromios the Boisterous come drifting down. Follow them cautiously to the high hill over the town whence you can see the Bad Stair, and for nearly two hours you may still see those lights before they vanish four thousand feet up. And what happened then?

Part of the answer is in the *Bacchae* of Euripides, but not all. For that play is not set in the chill of creeping winter, which these Athenian girls and women had to face in company with the Delphian Thyiads. The Corycian Cave, to which they climbed, is not easy of access nowadays—it is about three hours on foot from Delphi; but it is very large and a warm shelter in a storm;

[10] The only path up Parnassus from Delphi.

moreover wine in abundance could be stored in it. Once upon a time news came to Delphi that, before the Thyiads could reach the cave, they had been overwhelmed in a great snow blizzard, and the rescue-party which climbed up to look for them had all their clothing frozen stiff. Another time Thyiads lost their way one night after they had been ranging the mountain, and came down unwittingly to the township of Amphissa where the citizens found them next morning asleep from sheer exhaustion in the market-place. Such is the picture, so far as we can draw it, of the winter *orgia* in all their dire austerity, and the Athenian Thyiads knew only these; but there is other evidence for spring-time *orgia*, on the Corycian plain and round the sacred cave, when the Delphian Thyiads climbed the mountain without their Athenian sisters. Then there were goats to be milked in the flowered meadows, and the male participants with tied-on satyr-tails carried skins of wine. No doubt exists that at this season there was sexual freedom. Euripides in another play, the *Ion*, the scene of which is laid in Delphi, held it natural. The hero, Ion, considers it to be a convincing account of his birth, that his reputed father Xuthos came as a visitor to Delphi and took part with a throng of Thyiads in the Bacchic festival there.

ION: Did you stay in a hostel?

XUTHOS: Yes, and with Delphian girls.

ION: Do you mean you were one of their throng?

XUTHOS: They were maenad girls of Bacchos.

ION: Were you sober or wined?

XUTHOS: Under the pleasant influence of Bacchos.

ION: That indeed was my begetting.

But, along with this, one must ponder another passage from Euripides' *Bacchae*: "Dionysos compels no woman to be chaste. Chastity is a matter of character, and she who is naturally chaste will partake of Bacchic rites without being touched." Their state of *ecstasis* left the Bacchai free to follow either the instincts or the restraints of nature. No inhibitions stopped the satisfaction of desire; no exhibitionist urge drove them towards promiscuous folly. Even to the end, the cult of Dionysos was something of a mystic and terrifying incursion from the outside invisible world —an incursion from the dizzy heights beyond the limits of conscious personal men.[11]

Religious observances have throughout history produced many and startling acts such as appear inconsistent with the normal codes of a community. Yet the pilgrimage to Delphi of the Athenian Thyiads, which went on for many centuries was undoubtedly and exceptionally remarkable. In the framework of Athenian society it was for any family a great distinction when a young girl was chosen as a servitor of Athene on the Acropolis or as a processional basket-bearer in the Greater Panathenaic Festival. A father or a brother spoke with pride: "My little girl has been picked as an *arrephoros* for Athene." "My young sister is a *kanephoros* in this year's Festival."[12] But it is only fair to assume that in every second year a man might say to his friend: "The Priest of Dionysos has chosen my wife (*or* my daughter) to be a Thyiad this coming autumn. She's pretty tough of course, but I hope she can stand it." Did husband or father worry much lest the woman returned with child? In Greek literature I have not found any evidence that he would have treated such an occurrence as catastrophic; and once more we are driven to the conclusion that the ancient world—the Greek part certainly and the Roman part partially—seems to have taken the healthy episodes of sex in its stride. Post-Constantinian Europe, tainted by sexual revulsion, began to brood more and more on sex as something wildly wicked and dangerously desirable. The effects of this continue to taint us. Valuable as are the big studies—from Havelock Ellis to Hubert Benoit—of eroticism and the analysis of aspects of love, western mankind is still excessively preoccupied with the subject. Yet to the ancients it was no cause for brooding, but just a part, albeit to some of them the best part, of life; easy to attain and satisfy in moderation.

[11] K. Preisendanz, "Thyiaden" in Pauly, Wissowa, Kroll, *Real-Encyclopaedie*, Series II, Vol. VI, 1937; a long article which is the only modern full account of the Thyiads.

[12] See Seltman, *Women in Antiquity* (Pan Books), p. 104: (Thames and Hudson), pp. 119 f.

## Chapter Eight

## . . . AND SONG

IT now behoves us to record something about the many songs and glees, snatches and hymns associated with the use of wines. So far only two episodes have come up for reference. Socrates, in the *Symposium* written by Xenophon, being made aware of something in the conversation tending towards quarrelsomeness, tactfully said that it was time for a sing-song and himself started a glee.[1] In a story of much more recent date there was music and singing laid on at a modern rustic *taverna* for the treading of the grapes.[2]

Song is to be our theme; but before it is illustrated by some translations of ancient Greek verses, there are other forms of entertainment, such as were part of most convivial parties, to be borne in mind; especially since they happened not to occur during the very sober and elegant *symposium* given by Kallias to which Socrates came.

Frequently there was in the first place a game of skill called *kottabos*, which enjoyed great popularity for a very long time. In the second place most of such parties were less restrained than that which Kallias gave, and, as the night wore on, there was no lack of love-making.

Lastly the singing, which had a wide range. First come those

[1] See p. 8 above.
[2] See p. 80 above.

short songs which were truly hymns to individual gods and which accompanied the pouring of libations. Next one may mention political and patriotic songs, the most famous being one that has been called the national anthem of Athens. Third there are the simple drinking songs to be classed with modern efforts like "In cellar cool", or "Roll out the Barrel".

And fourth and finally the amorous songs, some of true grace, beauty and gaiety; others, also, only to be read in the original Greek, because their complete frankness must, in this prevailing civilisation of ours, be "veiled in the decent obscurity of an ancient language".

All the different kinds of songs were called *skolia*, a term very loosely used. Basically *skolion* was something that might be involved, twisted and perhaps contain hidden allusions; or it could be free of all ambiguity. The singer held a myrtle-branch and, when he had finished, passed the branch to another guest— acquaintance or girl-friend—calling on him or her for a song. These songs and glees were so diversified that they would weave into other happenings at a feast, and it will therefore be best to give some account of the *kottabos* game before providing a selection of the many *skolia* that survive. This required manual skill and was played in many different ways; the essential thing always was the discharge of the "heel-taps" of a bowl of wine at some mark. For this purpose an open bowl without a raised rim had to be employed; it was suspended by its handle on one finger, and its contents discharged by a sudden swing. The variety of the game depended upon the target that was used. Sometimes it was merely a disc set up on a stand like a candelabrum topped by a sphinx (Pl. XIII), or other figure; sometimes smaller bowls were floated in a larger one, and had to be filled; sometimes there was a scale which descended when properly hit, and struck an object below, often a little figure called "slave". Not only was correctness of aim required, but the sound with which the heel-tap struck the bowl or other object was a sign of skill, and was also taken as an augury, especially in love-matters, a name being pronounced with the throw. The game is frequently represented on vases.

The *kottabos*-player required some of the knack of a darts-player today, but he or she did not rise in their energy to toe a line, for they could rest gracefully upon the couch while the boy attendant moved the *kottabos*-stand into a convenient position ready for the quick flick of the wrist which might, or might not, drop the lees of wine onto the delicately balanced disc. A pleasing picture of a *hetaira*, or girl-friend, with her drinking-cup poised for the "shot" is on a vase by Phintias[3] painted about 500 B.C. She turns round to announce the name of the man for whom she is making the "throw". Sometimes there were forfeits in this game, as in "strip-poker". But this could not prove to be very profitable since the players of the game wore little or nothing anyhow.

*Skolia* might be sung after the main part of the dinner was over and when the drinks were changed. The *kottabos* stands were set up, the young flute-girl had warmed up her flutes and was playing an outlandish tune for the guests while another little wench with a triangular "Egyptian" lyre was singing to its accompaniment a bawdy little song.[4] When a pause came the host, perhaps, holding a branch of myrtle, would sing the first *skolion* to Zeus; one which was written by a famous poet, Ter-pander of Lesbos, who flourished about 676 B.C. It is a prayer, full of piety.

> Zeus, beginning of all things,
> Of all things the leader,
> Zeus, to thee a libation
> I pour, of hymns the beginning.[5]

About a century later someone composed a *skolion* to Athene, wherein there is felt to be a suble change, for the writer seems to have been a supporter of the Despot of Athens, Peisistratus, that ardent promoter of Athene's worship.

3 Seltman, *Women in Antiquity* (Pan Books), Fig. 12; (Thames and Hudson), Pl. XIII *a*.
4 Athenaeus, *The Sages at Dinner*, Book XV, 665 d.
5 *Oxford Book of Greek Verse in Translation*, No. 99, translation by Sir Maurice Bowra.

Pallas Tritogeneia Lady Athene,
Govern Thou this City and Thy citizens;
Keep us from suffering and from rebellion,
And from untimely death. To Thee
And to Thy Father Zeus we pray.

As a third hymn we may select a *skolion* for Demeter and Persephone, also of the sixth century B.C., which might have been composed in Eleusis, main centre of the cult of the Mother and Daughter goddesses, as well as of Ploutos, god of riches, or wealth.

I sing the Mother of Wealth, Olympian Goddess
Demeter, at this season when wreaths are worn.
And Thee too, daughter of Zeus, maiden Persephone.
Hail to You both; guard You our City well.

There seems an historical touch, if not a political allusion, in the neat little drinking song which was most probably composed just after the famous Athenian victory at Marathon in 490 B.C., for the *skolion* is for Pan whose cult the Athenians first established at that time. It is a celebrated story how—when the Medes landed on the beach at Marathon—Philippides, a famous runner, offered to take the news to distant Sparta, which had promised help. Resting in a cave in Arcadia he saw the god Pan, who reproached the Athenians for their neglect of his worship. "You will win," said the god, "but do not omit to give me a shrine." After the miraculous victory—for such it was—Philippides, who had fought in the battle, asked permission to take the great news to Athens. This, indeed, was the first "Marathon" run in the history of the world, and it has established in modern times the distance to be run. For the runner the strain was too great, but he got into the Athenian gate, cried out "our victory!" and dropped dead. But the people of Athens gave Pan a sacred grotto on the north slope of the Acropolis and composed this song.

O Pan, ruler over glorious Arcadia,
Dancer among the boisterous nymphs,
Laugh, O Pan, laugh gaily

At these merry songs of mine,
We won as we desired;
Ay, the gods gave victory.

No *skolion* in all ancient history was as famous as the song
called "The Harmodios". It celebrated a deed that stirred all
Hellas. Liberators, political assassins, vulgar feuders, what were
they? Singers, sculptors, and painters combined to raise Harmodios and his kinsman Aristogeiton to heroic stature, while
aristocrats and scandalmongers tried subtle calumniation. Brief
the story must be. The good despot Peisistratus who made Athens
great died peacefully in 527 B.C. and was succeeded by two of his
sons, Hippias and Hipparchos, who ruled jointly and ruled well.
Members of the leading family of the Athenian aristocrats—the
Alcmaeonidae—were in exile, some at Delphi, some in Boeotia
across the northern border, and they were intriguing for the
overthrow of the tyrant sons of the dead tyrant. During the sixth
century numerous aliens from other Greek States had come to
Athens to live and had acquired a kind of citizenship, among them
two members of a family called Gephyraioi which had left
Tanagra in Boeotia to settle on the banks of the Athenian
Cephissus. In 514 B.C. a conspiracy, its aim the killing of both
rulers, was formed by a number of nobles living in Athens and
the two Gephyraean kinsmen, Harmodios and Aristogeiton, were
enrolled as executioners. The whole plot may have been inspired
from Boeotia and by the exiled Alcmaeonidae waiting on the
frontier ready to enter and take over Athens when news of the
assassination should reach them.[6] But the plot failed; or, at best,
only half of it succeeded. At the Great Panathenaic Festival men
gathered in arms for the procession up to the Acropolis, and only
at such a time could the conspirators expect support from citizens.
The two kinsmen, armed with daggers hidden in myrtle branches
planned first to kill Hippias at one marshalling point for the procession, and then in the turmoil to escape and kill Hipparchos at

[6] This is in part my personal view of the background of the plot; but it
finds some support from the chief authority on the Athenian tyrants,
F. Cornelius, *Die Tyrannis in Athen* (Munich, 1929), pp. 82 ff.

another point. As the critical moment drew near, they saw one of
their fellow-conspirators talking to Hippias and thought they
were being betrayed. In panic they rushed to find Hipparchos
and killed him. Harmodios was cut down by the guards; Aristogeiton was taken alive. Put to the torture—since he could be
classed as an alien—he got his revenge by naming all Hippias'
best friends as fellow-conspirators.

When Athens was liberated and Hippias expelled in 510 B.C.
the two kinsmen began to be classed as heroes and as archetypal
Liberators. Bronze statues of the pair were made by a famous
sculptor, Antenor, and placed in the great Athenian market place.
The now successful Alcmaeonidae, democratically minded, pro-
fessed admiration, the *demos*—the populace—worshipped the
pair, but the old aristocrats and the secret friends of the tyrants
detested them. Accordingly derogatory stories began to obtain
circulation. Ancient histories frequently reveal an endeavour to
stress some form of sexual irregularity in the private lives of
famous people whom their opponents and detractors are anxious
to besmirch. Alexander's is the most obvious case, since his
enemies invented for him accusations of promiscuous excess
either with one sex or the other. Some among Alexander's
detractors raised another accusation—continence akin to neurotic
impotence—surely in the ancient world the most unkind cut
of all![7] The "great Liberator" rôle of the two Athenian kinsmen
was in after days minimised by some writers in search of something about their private lives to explain the act. First it was said
that Aristogeiton was the lover of Harmodios and that the despot
Hipparchos tried to oust him. Alternatively, Harmodios repulsed
the attentions of Hipparchos, and so the latter took his revenge
by debarring from the Panathenaic Procession as "unsuitable"
Harmodios' sister who had won the great distinction of a place
in the Festival. Such an act would admittedly have been a slur on
the whole family. But these stories with their vague sex involve-
ments do not accord with the fact that there were *other* conspirators. Men do not commit themselves to a dangerous murder

7 Seltman, *The Twelve Olympians and their Guests*, pp. 184 f.

plot in order to vindicate the honour of a young girl related to one of their number. There must be more than feuding behind it all, and the existence of other conspirators is the cogent factor. For most of the Athenian people the two Liberators seemed to be of heroic stature, and, because at every wine-party at which *skolia* were sung and a myrtle-branch passed round, the most popular song of all was the following: we may call it the "National Anthem of the Athenians".

> In a myrtle-branch I will carry my sword,
> Like Harmodios and Aristogeiton,
> When they slew the tyrant and made of Athens
> A city of equal rights.
>
> Harmodios, best of men, you are not dead, I know,
> But they say you are in the Islands,
> The Islands of the Blest, where dwell swift-foot Achilles,
> And Diomede, brave son of Tydeus.
>
> In a myrtle-branch I will carry my sword,
> Like Harmodios and Aristogeiton,
> When at the Feast of Athene
> They slew the tyrant Hipparchos.
>
> Ever shall your fame live in the earth,
> Harmodios, best of men, and Aristogeiton,
> For you slew the tyrant and made of Athens,
> A city of equal rights.

Harmodios and Aristogeiton were probably straightforward political assassins, bent, as countless Greeks had been, on freeing their country either from a Tyrant with a bodyguard, or from a Pasha and his Bashi-bazouks, or from a Field Marshal with Divisions at his beck and call. Such killers did, and still do, tend to stir the imagination and to win the admiration of the most intense individualists in history. Greek man has been—since Homer's day—and still is, a political animal.

Our disgression has run to some length, but this was unavoidable since one must needs explain the most popular of all drinking songs which contains no word about wine. Now, however, we may pass on to recite a few *skolia* concerned with wine and with cups.

First a brittle little piece by Alkman of Sparta written sometime around 600 B.C., named by the translator,[8] "The Footsteps of Spring".

> The flowery Spring—I heard her, coming upon her way,
> A bowl of honey-sweet wine! And mix it fast as ye may.

Anacreon of Lesbos wrote in the earlier part of the sixth century a ringing invocation to Hephaistos.[9]

> Moulding silver make for me, Hephaistos, no suit of armour,
> But fashion as deep as you can a hollow cup.
> Work on it neither stars nor chariots nor grim Orion,
> But blooming vines, laughing clusters and Bacchos, the fair god.

Since the days of Pythagoras, if not before, the Greeks appear to have had an urge for classification; and when, in the Hellenistic age, Librarianship as a calling was developed both in Alexandria and Pergamum the cataloguing of various literary forms became fairly stylised. Certain short poems were collected and classed as *skolia*, others as "Epigrams". The division was often artificial since it is apparent that, if you can set an "Epigram" to music and sing it, you have got a *skolion*. What actually occurred was that if there had been composed a *skolion* about love such as you sang at a feast with your eye on a girl-friend or on one of the little wantons, the later Librarians and pedants, like Athenaeus, carefully filed it among the "Amatory Epigrams". Yet it remains fairly obvious when these Epigrams are *skolia* as well. A neat one by Euenos, a fifth-century B.C. poet, runs as follows:

[8] F. L. Lucas, *Greek Poetry for Everyman*, p. 242.
[9] On whom see Seltman, *The Twelve Olympians*, Chapter VII.

The best measure of wine is neither much nor very little;
For 'tis the cause of either grief or madness.
It pleases the wine to be the fourth, mixed with three Nymphs.
Then too 'tis most suited for the bridal chamber and love.
But if it breathe too fiercely, it puts the Loves to flight,
And plunges men in a sleep, neighbour to death.[10]

In this little poem "Nymphs" mean water, and Euenos is subtly commending to lovers a mixture of three parts water to one of wine. That wine was clearly potent if taken neat.

Asklepiades of Samos, teacher of Theocritus, and a contemporary of Alexander the Great, seems to carry over the spirit of the older Hellenic to the young Hellenistic age. A drinking-song, perhaps of about 300 B.C., has a particularly felicitous translation.[11]

With Hermione the witching as I once played, she was wearing
A girdle of many colours, O Love, about her waist,
Broidered in golden letters—"Love me! Yet no despairing,
If you behold my beauty by a new love's arms enlaced".

Drink, drink, Asclepiades. What use to wail your sorrows?
Are you the first that Kypris beneath her heel hath thrust?
Your heart the first that felt how grim Love whets his arrows
And bends his bow for smiting? You live. Why gnaw the dust?
Come, pour the wine!—no water! Look, in the east, Dawn's finger!

Must we wait for the laggard lantern that bids men bedward creep?
Then here's a health, wan lover. Brief, brief our time to linger,
Poor fool, ere we are lying, night without end, asleep.

But from this elegance we may first look back; then forward: back to the splendid vitality of the fifth-century man and his girl.

---

[10] There is a curious parallelism between the dainty thought in this poem and the rollicking bawdiness of the Porter in *Macbeth*, Act II, Scene iii.

[11] F. L. Lucas, *op. cit.*, pp. 318 f.

Drink with me,
Sport with me,
Love with me,
Crown your head with me,
Rage with me when I rage,
And, when I'm calm, be calm!

No name for the author of that exciting song.

And now forward to the first century B.C. at a repentant but nostalgic little piece by Philodemus who lived in Rome and Naples.

I wish no garlands of white violets again.
No lyre-playing again, no Chian wine again,
No Syrian myrrh again, no revelling again,
No thirsty strumpet here again; for I hate what leads to madness.

Bind my head with narcissus and pass the crooked flute,
Anoint my limbs with saffron and wet my gullet with wine of Mytilene.
Then mate me with a virgin who will love her nest.

Philodemus, though he had a Greek name, was a Gadarene of Palestine, and may have had some Semitic blood. Anyhow those few verses seem to carry prohibitions fit for a Decalogue and a real touch of the repetitive beauty in Hebrew poetry.

Three more short poems of about 300 B.C. by the felicitous Asklepiades of Samos, merit quotation. The first might be aimed at a lovelorn man; the second could be sung by a girl-friend taking part in a symposium.

Wine is the proof of love.
Nikagoras denied he was in love,
But all those toasts convicted him.
Yes! he shed tears and bent his head,
And looked all downcast,
While the wreath around his head
Drooped all awry.

> Once Archeades loved to sit close to me,
> But now not even in play, unhappy me,
> Does he turn round to look at me,
> Honeyed Eros is not forever sweet,
> But often when tormenting lovers,
> Becomes a sweeter god.

In either case the singer could change the name as it now stands in the song, provided its syllables would fit in.

The third little poem by Asklepiades is not clearly a *skolion*, but it cannot fail to suggest that party atmosphere in which the young girl-friend is dressed up in one of the boys' hat and cloak.

> Young Dorkis loves to sport with the lads
> And knows how to shoot, like a gentle boy,
> The swift dart of Cyprian Pandemos,[12]
> Flashing desire from her eye.
> Under her boyish hat (the long hair falls)
> Over her gleaming shoulders.
> And the short cloak shows her naked thigh.

Poseidippos, who was a contemporary of the Samian poet, wrote more than one piece for women. A prayer to Aphrodite from a wanton courtesan named Kallistion, or "Little Lovely":

> Goddess who hauntest Cyprus
> And Cythera and Miletus
> And the fair plain of Syria echoing to horses' hooves,
> Come graciously to Kallistion,
> Who's never turned a lover from her door.

Mixing the wine and water at a Symposium is clearly a drinking song, a *skolion* with slightly intricate allusions in it.

Mimnermus, who wrote about 650 B.C., had a girl-friend called Nanno, while Antimachus, another elegiac poet, of the mid-fifth century B.C., had a girl called Lydé. Poseidippos, writer of the

---

[12] That is "Aphrodite of the whole People", her favourite title in Athens. See Seltman, *The Twelve Olympians* (Pan Books), p. 84; (Max Parrish), pp. 84 f. The words in brackets in line 5 of this poem are my attempt to fill a lacuna, or gap.

next *Skolion*, imagines himself in their company with his boy, Heliodoros, who is mixing the wine. This poem is of course archaising, and so a little artificial; but amusing none the less.

> Pour in two ladles for Nanno and Lydé,
> One for the lover, Mimnermus, one for wise Antimachus,
> And with the fifth mix in myself, Heliodoros.
> With the sixth say, "for everyone who ever chanced to love".
> Say the seventh is for Hesiod, the eighth for Homer,
> The ninth for the Muses, and the tenth for Memory.
> I drink the bowl full to the brim, Cypris,
> To thee and to all the other Loves.

Just what proportions are here intended remains obscure though one could venture a guess that the ladles for the two girls, the Muses and Memory are from the water-jar, those for the two poets, the writer, Hesiod and Homer and "all lovers" are drawn from the wine. That would make six parts of wine to four of water, a possible mixture.

By the first century B.C. men were still writing drinking songs and epigrams on wine and women. Anxiety was in the air, wars and civil wars were plaguing the world, and men felt jaded, as the next three poems show.

Antipater, of Sidon in Phoenicia, wrote in the first century B.C. His verses are addressed to Seleucus, and this could be the last king of that name who ruled over Syria and Phoenicia from 96 to 94 B.C. However, it need not have been King Seleucus VI, but some other worthless scion of that once famous House.

Men learned in the stars say I'm short-lived.
I am, Seleucus, but I care not.
There is one road down to Hades for all,
And if mine's quicker, I shall see Minos all the sooner.
Let us drink; for this is very truth, that wine is a horse for the road,
While foot-travellers take a stony-path to Hades.

Antipater will go by the royal road mounted on "Wine".
Pedestrian abstainers, wineless, will reach Hades just the same.

Frustration is there too in the mind of Philodemus, one of whose drinking songs has already been cited.[13]

Demo and Thermion are killing me.
Thermion's a strumpet; Demo a girl who knows not Cypris yet.
The one I fondle; the other I may not.
By Thy holy Self, Cypris, I swear, I know not which to call the more
    desirable.
Little Demo I'll say, the virgin, for I don't really want what's ready to
    hand,
But I long for whatever's kept under close restraint.

Even Marcus Argentarius, an Augustan poet, Latin in name, but writing his verses in Greek, has not really lost that sense of the purposeless quality of life, although Augustus had given the world new hope.

Dead, five feet of earth shall be yours.
You'll not look on the delights of life nor on the rays of the sun.
So take the cup of unmixed "Bacchos", Cincius, and drain it
Rejoicing with your arm round your lovely mistress.

Epigrams and *skolia* were to entice the pens of poets for more than another six centuries before they faded away under the pressing solemnities of the Church. So continuous a flow of neat, brief, little, samples of versification could achieve scarcely any originality. Perhaps the form might have faded into oblivion but for the passions of two remarkable men.

Strato of Sardis, where Lydian laxity lingered on down to the reign of Hadrian and beyond, produced about one hundred epigrams incorporated in Book XII of the *Greek Anthology*. Almost all are about homosexual love. "Coarse or mawkish", "neither sociologically nor aesthetically interesting"; the verdict of Professor Highet commands assent.[14] But if these verses had not been popular their author would not have churned them out as he did. Homosexuality, never absent, is more fashionable during certain periods than during others. When it is in fashion

[13] See p. 119 above.
[14] *O.C.D.*, p. 864.

its advocates and practitioners indulge an ardent search, as Strato did, for precedent and parallel in the past. And Strato had example and, almost certainly, encouragement from the highest quarters. Neither Antony's devotion to Cleopatra, nor that of Claudius to Messalina, nor the love of Nero for Poppaea could compare with the overpowering passion of the Emperor Hadrian for that perfect boy, Antinous.[15] Hadrian's discovery of the youth, his open display of his love; the young man's early death by drowning in the Nile, his deification—ephemeral though it was—combined with a good emperor's bitter grief to give a passing sheen of popularity to all poems about pretty youths. Strato's collection remains, for a majority of those who have read it, the most tedious, sniggering patch by far in all Greek literature, and, though frequent mention of wine occurs it will suffice to record this fact, and to pass on.

Nearly four and a half centuries later there flourished the other passionate epigrammatist, a man far more remarkable than Strato. Paul the Silentiary was at the height of his powers about A.D. 560 in the reign of Justinian the Great, most powerful of all Byzantine Emperors. His ancestors were illustrious, he inherited great wealth, and was Chief of the Silentiarii or Secretaries of State of the Emperor. Poetry was his passion, and the Christian half of his genius produced an architectural epic, of more than a thousand lines, which was a detailed description of that incomparable masterpiece Hagia Sophia, the Church of the Holy Wisdom in Constantinople. But the pagan half of Paul's genius turned out the last fine flourish of Greek Epigrams, eighty-three in all, many of which might have served as *skolia* sung in the dining hall of one of his own fine palaces or villas.

Wine-drinkers, we shall pour a libation to laughter—waking Bacchos,
With cups and more cups we'll expel man-killing care.
Let the toiling rustic fill his barley-soaked belly with beer—gift of the
    mother of black-robed Persephone,

---

[15] See *C.A.H.*, xi, p. 791; Seltman, *A.G.A.*, p. 112; Seltman, *The Twelve Olympians* (Max Parrish), p. 195.

To wild beasts and birds that tear raw flesh we will leave the copious
   and bloody meat of slain bulls.
Give fish-bones, that cut the skin, to the lips of men to whom Hades is
   dearer than the sun.
But for us let wine the bountiful be ever food and drink, and let others
   long for this ambrosia.

The Greek of this is highly intricate as a *skolion* should be.
Translation is difficult and I have taken a liberty by inserting
beer, because it makes a better pattern: wine, beer, blood, wine.
To put bread instead of beer is illogical and pedestrian. The
"mother of black-robed Persephone" is Demeter goddess of
corn, and from barley-corn they made beer in Thrace, close to the
walls of Constantinople; though that country was even more
noted for its famous wines.

Forty of the surviving epigrams of Paul the Silentiary are
frankly erotic and generally lively and entertaining. That is a
remarkable phenomenon for the times and one cannot but wonder
how this great man managed to square his amorous practices and
fancies with his lip-service to a faith shot through and through
with prohibitions.

Five of his little poems, which might be sung to the various
girls who frequented his parties, will suffice to make the point.

Let's steal our kisses, Rhodope,
And the lovely—the precious—work of Aphrodite Cypris.
It is sweet not to be found out;
Sweet to avoid the all-entrapping eyes of guardians:
Furtive amours are more honied than open ones.

From her golden head Doris pulled one hair and bound my hands
   with it,
Myself her prisoner, at first I laughed, thinking it easy to loose her
   lovely fetter.
But finding I'd no strength to break it, soon I began to moan,
Like one held tight by iron bonds. And now, unhappy me,
Hung on a hair, I must follow ever where my mistress wills.

Galatea's kisses are long and smack,
Demo's are soft, and Doris bites me.
Which excites most? Let not ears judge kisses;
I'll taste the three and vote. My heart, you were wrong;
You knew already Demo's soft kiss and the sweet honey of her fresh
    mouth.
Cleave to that; she wins without a bribe.

Let us throw off these clothes, my pretty one, and lie naked,
Knotted in each other's embrace. Nothing between us;
Even that thin tissue you wear seems thick to me as the walls of
    Babylon.
Let our breasts, our lips be linked; the rest veiled in silence.
I hate a babbling tongue.

I hold her breasts in my hands, our lips are joined;
And I feed in passion unrestrained round her silver neck,
But not yet is my conquest complete; for I still toil, wooing.
A girl who refuses me her bed. Half of herself
She has given to Aphrodite, half to Athene;
And I, between the two, I waste away.

All things considered Paul the Silentiary remains an enigma,
the last poetic genius of the ancient Greek world; for in the
original some of his stuff is very good indeed. And yet he was
a man left over from an earlier and happier age, a man who could
give gay wine-parties for his elegant friends and his lovely little
girls, and—because of his enormous prestige—get away with it
even in the age of the pious Justinian. But long before his day
repressive mental conflict was agonising too many minds. The
other and earlier Paul—he of Tarsus—brilliant and gifted, was
what we call today a Fundamentalist, believing in the historicity
of "the Fall", and the especial sinfulness of woman through Eve.
Those who followed, whether we now call them orthodox or
heretical, grew to deplore sex. Mani, who taught in the mid-third
century of our era and called himself "Apostle of Jesus Christ",
conceived a hatred of material creation.[16] This attitude passed

[16] See especially Steven Runciman, *The Mediaeval Manichee*, Chapter II.

centuries later by way of the Manichees of Provence into the love poetry of that country, and the troubadours held both marriage and the mutual happiness of lovers in contempt. By this twelfth-century attitude too many western men and women are still contaminated.[17]

Sin and sex were already closely linked in a poem written by a contemporary and close friend of Paul the Silentiary, Agathias Scholasticus. Guiltiness had won its victory over sober sense.

> May Aphrodite herself and the darling Loves
> Melt my empty heart for hate of me,
> If ever I'm inclined to love males. May I never
> Make such conquests or fall into the graver sin.
> It is enough to sin with women, and this I'll do.
> But leave young men to foolish Pittalokos.

Here is something really new in poetry. There had been Greeks who preferred homosexual love, and more Greeks who sought the heterosexual delights. It was entirely a matter of personal preference; no questions asked; no comments made. It was laughable that a notion of "sin" should intrude.[18] But mediaeval Christendom was building another structure, and an age of cowled repression was in store for a foolish world.

Just how far have the young men and women of our day got away from the morbidities of their ancestors? Many certainly have; otherwise we should not encounter such wise and hopeful studies on reasonable attitudes to sex as continue to get into print. L. S. Feuer's[19] brilliant recent work, which contradicts certain assumptions of Freud, justifies by reasoned argument moral principles which are both biologically and attractively hedonistic. Human conduct should express as many desires, and repress as few, as possible. Basic needs are food and sex. Psycho-

---

[17] See Denis de Rougemont, *Passion and Society*.

[18] On sin see Seltman, *The Twelve Olympians* (Pan Books), p. 23; (Max Parrish), pp. 27 f.

[19] L. S. Feuer, *Psycho-analysis and Ethics* (Springfield, Illinois and Blackwell, Oxford).

analysis must reveal to us what our basic desires are, whereupon
—always in moderation, lest we spoil the pattern of things—we
should act upon them. Sexual satisfaction, Professor Feuer main-
tains, adds to the cultural energy of human beings. And this, of
course, whether or no he is aware of it, is a restatement of Hellenic
humanism.

The little poem of Agathias Scholasticus is sadness indeed. We
must not leave it at that, closing a chapter in the fog of sin-damped
Christendom. Rather let us recover our own balance and fling
back to the sixth century B.C., to the early masters of Liberty,
Moderation, and Sound Sense. First hear Alcaeus singing of wine
and girls; and, after him, Anacreon—a mild Petruchio—talking
to his pretty Thracian slave-girl.[20]

> Soak your lungs with wine, for now
> The Dog Star's at the turn.
> How the summer wounds, and how
> All must thirst and burn.
>
> In the bushes, strong and clear
> Now the cricket sings,
> And sweet music fills the air
> From beneath his wings.
>
> Now is all the earth at song
> In the summer's fire,
> And the girasole is strong.
> Now does wild desire
>
> Make the girls most amorous,
> But the men won't please;
> For the fire of Sirius
> Withers heads and knees.

[20] *Oxford Book of Greek Verse in Translation*, pp. 202 and 222 f. Translations by C. M. Bowra and Walter Headlam.

Ah tell me why you turn and fly,
My little Thracian filly shy?
Why turn askance
That cruel glance,
And think that such a dunce am I?

O I am blest with ample wit
To fix the bridle and the bit,
And make thee bend
Each turning-end
In harness all the course of it.

But now 'tis yet the meadow free
And frisking it with merry glee;
The master yet
Has not been met
To mount the car and manage thee.

*Chapter Nine*

✤✦✤✦✤✦✤✦✤✦✤✦✤✦✤✦✤✦✤✦✤✦✤✦✤✦✤✦✤✦✤✦✤✦✤✦✤✦✤✦

# THE TRADE

✤✦✤✦✤✦✤✦✤✦✤✦✤✦✤✦✤✦✤✦✤✦✤✦✤✦✤✦✤✦✤✦✤✦✤✦✤✦✤✦

NOT an ocean. A sea—not quite land-locked but nearly so, the Mediterranean is the biggest lake in the world fed by another vast lake—the Black Sea—like some great liquid cistern filling the Midland Main. As the St Lawrence River runs to the Atlantic through the Great Lakes of North America, so the River of Bosphorus and Hellespont, running between Kythera and Antikythera, passes by Malta and Gibraltar into Ocean.

Around the shores of this great sea there seems to be a remarkable unity of formation, landscape, colour, light—a unity expressed in happy variety. Memories crowd in. A little blue bay at Vouliagmeni on the south coast of Attica; its pale, pink, bony rocks cupped between hills, green with pine trees by the sea. Farther back are the little stubby vines and the grey olive boles. Solitary palm-trees sway their tops in a passing breeze. Earth, red with ruddle, marble-white rock where last winter's frost broke a fresh gash into the sparkling limestone. Pines, olives, vines, and in spring a shining carpet thick with flowers. Further inland are the hard mountains cut out against that deep blue noonday sky, from which the sunlight falls; such light in which the human skin draws life—a new sensation passing into the flesh beneath—until a being may feel itself transmuted by some unexplained power into another, more god-like creature.

And then the islands. Not so much the great islands, Corsica,

Sardinia, Sicily, Crete, Rhodes, Cyprus; but the lesser ones which
—as the light strikes through the water at their edges—seem
undercut, and one perceives how men once thought that certain
islands floated on the sea. In the Aegean, the Archipelago itself,
the height of beauty is attained.

As you sail over that liquid taffeta sea the islands take their positions
like dancers and move away and together. As the ship's wake churns
vigorously out from beneath you they dance a pavanne afar off; circling
in dreamy attendance on the exhilarating solo of your vessel as they
weave their spell. . . . A State of wondering personal adventure is made
the more intense by the alchemy of the light which shines on the
Aegean. It is a light which has always amazed travellers because, as it
changes, it seems rather to alter the substances of what it illumines and
not, as other lights do, merely to reveal fresh aspects of the same things.
It creates colours which permeate the texture of the thing lit. . . . Again
in the evening light there is the overwhelming sense of magic at work.
There are more islands too, rocks of wild beauty scattered on the sea's
surface bearing such names as Donoussa, Kouphos, Skinoussa,
Heraklea and Despotiko. But you see these islands about you dimly.
The sun is low by now and those to the westward are blurred by the
haze of light streaming over them, those to the east are pale and
ethereal. Then the sun sinks beyond the point of dazzle, the colours
change as their substance becomes opaque and their outlines sharpen.
Far off pink and jewel-like cliffs are illumined, the light scintillates
along the grey-green scrub on the hills like very distant damask. The
shadows deepen and lie in drifts of blue and purple in the hollows, the
western islands turn black before the blue pall of darkness is drawn
across the sea. A last flutter of sharp excitement in the fading day is a
school of dolphins leaping at the prow.[1]

That is how we may see things now, and it has since Homer's
day been thus that men have seen them. From the Greek cities of
Gaul; Marseilles, Antibes, Nice—once Massalia, Antipolis, Nicaea
—to Ischia, Naples, Sorrento, Capri, Paestum and down the long
Greek Italian coasts; from all the splendid realms of Hellenic
Sicily, over to Corfu and the other islands of the Ionian Sea,
there pulses still that magical union of Nature and Humanity out

[1] C. Kininmonth, *The Children of Thetis*, pp. 30 ff.

of whose ecstatic intercourse our very civilisation is born. No wonder that the Midland Sea remains the irresistible magnet to draw men and women from bundling between the damp sheets of Europe's North to the hot naked sands of foam-born Aphrodite and to the loves of the immortal gods.

Greece, and the far-flung settlements of Greeks all over the Mediterranean littoral away from urban and industrial regions looked very much as they do now. But two things that the earlier Greeks never knew have arrived to change certain parts of the landscape—oranges and lemons, fruits that would have found great favour in the ancient world.

When one contemplates the relatively simple, but well-planned economic organisations of those distant times one becomes aware of the dominant parts played by three exportable commodities—corn, oil and wine. Lest we become side-tracked into a variety of interesting topics, we must now decide to concentrate only on the third of these commodities; and we may bear in mind that wine was quite as important as the others. Beside Demeter's corn and Athene's oil, the wine of Dionysos could fill a place of distinction. Enlightenment on the wine trade comes from two sources: late literati, and contemporary coins. Once an organised cultivation and export of wine has been built up, the *connoisseur* emerged to sample brands, vintage and proof, as well as to pontificate on *bouquet* and *arrière-goût*. Such a one was the learned Athenaeus. His encyclopaedic, but rambling, work called *The Sages at Dinner*—another translation of the Greek title is *The Gastronomers*—took long to write, for it appears to have been started before A.D. 200, and to have been completed soon after A.D. 228. From the first Book and the twenty-fifth section onwards, references to wines of many kinds are introduced, and the full catalogue of drink gets under way. Obviously the extensive repertoire of themes discussed make Athenaeus' production one of the most important Greek works of later antiquity that survive. For his long list of wines he drew more on older written sources than on his personal experience of the various drinks; we cannot therefore be sure that every *cru* to which he referred was still obtainable around A.D. 200. But Athenaeus was the great prototype of pedants; and it won a man more credit to be a literary know-all than to be a *degustateur*. Not that the two were mutually exclusive, then as now; though today such people have grown very rare.

The list of famous wine-growing regions mentioned in *The Sages at Dinner* contains much repetition, since, because there are many quotations, place-names recur. Notable for their popularity were the wines of Chios, Thasos, Lesbos, Peparethos, Mende, Icaria, Euboea, Naxos, Rhodes, Corcyra, and all these places bore on their coins symbols of the export trade which was of such obvious importance to their economic stability. The powerful states of the Greek world, most of them, grew vines of their own; but it was presumably all for home consumption, and there is no record of wine exported for general use by Athens, Sparta, Corinth or Syracuse. But all the nine states and cities just mentioned, as well as numerous others, took the trouble between the sixth and the second centuries B.C. to advertise their produce. Specimens of some of their coins (Pl. XIV) are of exceptional beauty.

When a man or a company of people wish to draw the attention of masses of other people to themselves, their theories or their products, they must find some means of conveying what they wish to convey quickly, as well as far and wide. Before the invention of the first printing-press, there was only one kind of "printed" matter capable of being quickly spread abroad, and that was coinage. Once Peisistratus, ruler of Athens in the sixth century B.C., had started to use the types invented for Athenian silver coins in order to emphasize the greatness of Athens, protected by the goddess Athene, the idea of printed, or minted, propaganda began to operate. Centuries later, Republican Romans, followed by the line of Imperial Rulers of the ancient world, would grasp the possibility of using the types and the inscriptions on current coin to disseminate the notions that they wished their followers and subjects to absorb. This was propaganda, and—as historians perceive ever more clearly—propaganda of a most efficient kind. It could be used to serve commercial as well as political or dynastic ends. Though only some Greek states used their coin types, or part of them, to call attention to exportable wares, they are not hard to recognise. The Macedonian and Thessalian plains were famed for rearing horses; the same districts, as well as Euboea, Crete and South Italy, were rich in cattle; the last province, with Sicily, Chalcedon and the Crimea, all owned wide corn-lands; olive-oil came from Attica, Crete, Samos, Aeolis and elsewhere. In every instance cited, there frequently appears on the coinage of the state a whole picture, or an adjunct type, referring to its special product.

The wine-trade, however, seems to have been more keenly advertised on coinage than any other; and if, as is possible, considerable competition between wine-growers existed, there would be an additional inducement to remind the whole world of men who handled coins about the merits of the wine one grew. A survey of "wine-coins" might extend as far west as Sicilian Naxos on the slopes of Etna, and as far east as the Black Sea coast, where Trapezus (Trebizond) (Pl. XIV) minted coins having for type a table laden with a huge bunch of grapes. But more can be learned from concentration upon a limited area—the Aegean Sea, its shores and islands (Figs. 21, 22). Here, in word and picture, automatically distributed to myriads of prospective purchasers, was something akin to competitive commercial advertising. But a touch of piety was present, too; for this superb wine was, after all, the gift of Dionysos to mankind. Had we included in our list other States which displayed a head of or a figure of the god, our catalogue would have been even longer.

Material evidence of the extent of the wine trade is plentiful, since the great amphorae which contained famous vintages, were marked by the application of seals impressed on their handles or their stoppers. For the well-known Rhodian brand two seals were in use; some being stamped with the head of the sun-god Helios, others with the heraldic rose of Rhodes; and these badges are identical with the types of the State's coinage. Alongside these circular badges were oblong stamps, bearing the name of an official and the month when the wine was bottled. At Thasos, rectangular stamps carried the name of the vintner, a registration mark, and the word Thasion, "of the Thasians", and a number of similar vintage marks for other States are recorded. Rhodian amphorae have been found in quantities at Alexandria and Cnidian amphorae, such as regularly appear on the coinage,

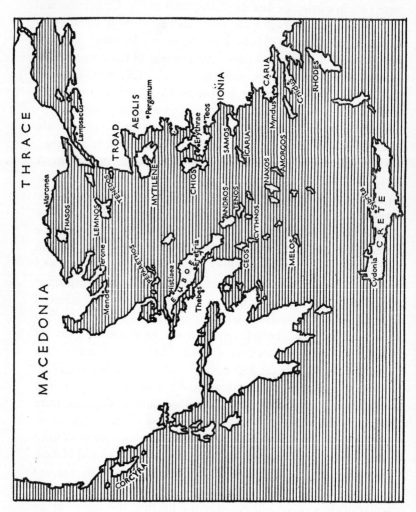

Fig. 22. COIN TYPES OF WINE STATES IN THE AEGEAN REGIONS

| State | Grapes | Wine-cup | Amphora |
|---|---|---|---|
| Mende (A) | x | x | x |
| Terone | x | x | — |
| Maronea (A) | x | — | — |
| Peparethos (A) | x | x | — |
| Thasos (A) | — | x | x |
| Lemnos (A) | x | — | — |
| Lampsacus (A) | — | x | x |
| Troad | x | x | x |
| Pergamum | x | — | — |
| Aeolis | x | x | x |
| Tenedos | x | — | — |
| Lesbos (A) | — | x | x |
| Erythrae (A) | x | — | — |
| Teos | x | x | x |
| Chios (A) | x | x | x |
| Samos | — | — | x |
| Icaria (A) | x | x | x |
| Cnidus (A) | x | — | x |
| Myndus (A) | x | — | — |
| Rhodes (A) | x | — | — |
| Euboea (A) | x | — | — |
| Thebes | x | x | x |
| Andros | — | x | x |
| Tenos | x | — | — |
| Ceos (A) | x | — | — |
| Cythnos | x | — | — |
| Naxos (A) | x | x | — |
| Melos (A) | — | x | x |
| Amorgos | — | x | x |
| Cydonia | x | — | — |
| Sybrita | x | — | — |

*Note:* (A) after the State's name denotes that it was known to Athenaeus as a wine producer.

travelled far, handles with the impressed stamp of Cnidus having been discovered in Sicily, Athens, Alexandria and at Olbia by the mouth of the Dnieper; while a whole vase with a Corcyraean vintage mark was found in a house at Pompeii. Pictures of ships carrying wine also survive, the oldest perhaps on a broken Corinthian terracotta tablet of about 600 B.C.[2] which shows part

[2] P. N. Ure, *The Origin of Tyranny*, p. 242, Fig. 35.

of a ship, and vases in the air above it, meant to represent the cargo. This may be a shipment of vases; but, where pots were transported, jars of wine would also travel. Much later is a mosaic at Tebessa in Roman North Africa, depicting a ship-load of amphorae. Best, however, is the real thing found and recorded on the floor of the Mediterranean sea. Before the last war there was observed an ancient wreck, twenty fathoms down, off the small harbour of Albenga on the Italian Riviera. Equipment designed for raising great weights from the sea-bed was employed; and, since this had the violent effect of a bulldozer, the ancient ship broke up, but not before there had been recovered a variety of utensils, as well as a cargo of seven hundred amphorae of wine. Since then, modern methods have developed fast; and off the Côte d'Azur, at Anthéon in the roads at Agay, men of the new profession—underwater archaeologists—have discovered at ten fathoms depth another wreck identified as of the first century B.C., which also carried a large cargo of wine-amphorae. Philippe Diolé, in *The Undersea Adventure*, has described them lying on the tideless bed "in the blue half-light of under-water". Others have recently been found by fishermen from Skiathos off Cape Artemision. One such (Pl. XV) is here illustrated.

Wine in ancient Greece was not expensive and anyone today who likes good wine must be moved to envy when he learns how cheap it generally was. Before proceeding to quote recorded prices it will, however, be best to set out a simple table of liquid measures as used both in Athens and in Macedonia and consequently in various parts of the Hellenistic world.3

    1 Kyathos (about 3 tablespoonfuls);
    6 Kyathoi = 1 Kotylé (nearly half a pint);
    12 Kotylai = 1 Chous ($5\frac{3}{4}$ to 6 pints)4;
    12 Choes = 1 Amphoreus Metrétés.

3 Other Greek states had different systems of liquid, as of dry, measures; but not very much is known about them.

4 Chous is pronounced like the Scottish "hoose" (*anglice* "house") with a very soft "K" sound on the front of it. A chous would go into a small sized painted amphora or into a pelike. My equivalents in pints, litres and gallons are, of course, only approximations.

Accordingly one Amphoreus Metrétés contained 12 Choes, 144 Kotyloi, 864 Kyathoi. The Amphoreus held 39·39 litres or 69·33 pints, or slightly over 8½ gallons. It may generally be assumed that the great pointed pottery jars in which wines were preserved, exported and sold were, each of them, such an amphoreus.

It is far from easy to translate monetary values of the ancient world into terms of modern cash. Only one gauge is useful, and that is the daily wage of an unskilled labourer. If such an one earned half adrachma a day one may equate it with about twenty-four shillings at the present time, and this, up to a point, is in accord with the contemporary cost of living.

The price of home-grown wine in Athens was four drachmas for the Metrétés, that is about 144 shillings for 8 to 9 gallons. This, at a time when the cost of living was high in Athens. In the sixth and early fifth centuries B.C. we may assume one-half of such a sum as the average. In the fourth century B.C. Demosthenes referred to 3000 jars of Mendaean wine, which was held to be, both in Macedonia and Athens, a very fine vintage, as worth six hundred drachmas. It is possible that this can be estimated as a little more than sixpence a gallon! Later on in the Hellenistic and Roman Republican age the famous wine from Lusitania—perhaps from the regions of Oporto—was astonishingly cheap, since 10 gallons were sold for the equivalent of ninepence.

Every traveller in Greece who visits places away from the beaten track knows how cheap local wine can be today. In the early thirties of the present century when the value of the paper drachma was very low the cost of wine, and of the local spirit, ouzo—often home-distilled from the skins of the trodden grapes—was astonishing in terms of the pound or dollar. In the spring of 1934 I arranged for a trip for five people from Olympia, where we had been staying, to Andritsaena in Arcadia. Not a long hard walk, for we followed the northern bank of the river Alpheus upstream for about twelve miles and crossed to the south bank by a ferry, near the point where the rivers Erymanthus and Diagon feed the Alpheus. Our Olympian guide made our party up to six, and his pony had to swim the river behind the ferry-boat. Climbing into the Arcadian mountains for about another six miles we came to a lonely village of some size called Zacha. From this place to Andritsaena a rough but unfinished road existed twenty-five years ago, and our host to be, who ran a bug-less guest-house at Andritsaena, and who was named Ambariotis was there to meet us with a van and his nephew as driver. We were now a party of eight seated on rickety chairs outside the village taverna where we invited the owner to drink with us. Since our walk was over we could relax; and we began with seven ouzos for the seven men, and two tumblers of an admirable local rose-red wine, slightly resinated, for the two women in our party. This was followed by a round of the rose retsina for everyone—another nine tumblers full—not little wine glasses. Presently I asked for the bill—seven ouzos, eleven tumblers of wine; but I was restrained by a gesture from Ambariotis, who said, "When I come to England you pay for my wine; but here in Arcadia I pay all yours."

Without too obvious a look I happened to see how much he did pay. At the rate of exchange between the pound and the drachma in 1934, a calculation showed it to be, for all those drinks, the equivalent of twopence halfpenny.

Authorities studied and quoted by Athenaeus clearly knew much more about the wine-trade in the Aegean area than about the production and export of wine among the western Greeks. But the latter did use their coinage to advertise the fact that they and their cities took pride in their wines, as a Map and Table (Figs. 23, 24 designed on the lines of Figs. 21, 22) may show. Yet though nineteen important states appear on our list, only four of them were referred to by Athenaeus as notable for their wine. And he actually omitted the best of them all—the cities of Naxos and Tauromenium on the southern and eastern slopes of Mount Etna. Volcanic soil—whether at Thera, or round Vesuvius, or on the long reaches descending from the great Etnaean massif—produces very fine wine.

The varied colours of wine in the ancient world were, as far

Fig. 23. Map of South Italy and Sicily showing certain wine-growing states.

as we can tell, similar to those which are produced today. Greeks recognised three colours; Romans four. For the former it was red (*melas*); white, that is pale straw-colour (*leukos*); and brown or amber-coloured (*kirrhos*). Romans distinguished four: *albus* answering to *leukos*, *fulvus* to *kirrhos*; while *melas* was sub-divided into *sanguineus* and *niger*, the former being doubtless applied to bright glowing wines like Burgundy, while the *niger* or *ater* would resemble Port. In modern Greek red wine is called *krasi mavro* or *oinos mavro*. In the ordinary Greek authors the epithet *erythros* is as common as *melas* and will represent the *sanguineus*. Among the ancients recourse was had to various

| Fig. 24. Coin Types of Wine States in Western Greek Regions | | | |
|---|---|---|---|
| *State* | *Grapes* | *Wine-cup* | *Amphora* |
| Cales (*A*) | – | x | – |
| Neapolis (*A*) | x | – | – |
| Tarentum (*A*) | x | x | x |
| Uxentum | – | x | – |
| Metapontum | x | – | – |
| Croton | – | x | – |
| Hipponium | – | – | x |
| Terina | – | – | x |
| Akragas (*A*) | x | – | – |
| Calacte | x | – | – |
| Camarina | – | – | x |
| Catana | x | – | – |
| Entella | x | – | – |
| Galaria | x | – | – |
| Hybla | – | x | – |
| Naxos | x | x | – |
| Sergetion | x | – | – |
| Tauromenium | x | – | – |
| Tyndaris | x | – | – |

*Note:* (*A*) after the State's name denotes that it was known to Athenaeus as a wine producer.

devices for preventing or correcting acidity, heightening the flavour, and increasing the durability of the inferior kinds of wine. This subject was reduced to a regular system by the Greeks. Pliny mentions four authors who had written formal treatises, and the authors of the Geoponic collection, together with Cato, Varro and Columella, supply a multitude of precepts upon the same topic. The object in view was accomplished sometimes by merely mixing different kinds of wine together, but more frequently by throwing into the amphorae various condiments or seasonings (*artuseis, conditurae*). When two wines were mixed together, those were selected which possessed opposite good qualities and defects, even as the cheaper Hocks of today are mixed with a high percentage of Italian white wines. Connoisseurs, however, justly valued most those wines which needed no such treatment. No foundation whatever exists for the supposition that the finest Greek wines, especially the products of the islands in the Aegean and Ionian Seas, belonged for the most part to the luscious sweet class. The very reverse is proved by the epithets *austeros*, *skleros*, *leptos* and the like, applied to a great number, while *glukus* and *glukazōn* are designations comparatively rare, and the ancients appear to have been fully sensible that sweet wines could not be swallowed either with pleasure or safety, except in small quantities. The mistake has arisen from not perceiving that the expressions *oinos glukus* and *oinos hēdus* are by no means necessarily synonymous. The former signifies wine positively sweet, the latter wine agreeable to the taste from the absence of acidity, in most cases indicating nothing more than sound wine.

Roman taste did not, apparently, take kindly to the wines of Etruria. Vineyards on the Vatican hill outside the northern boundaries of ancient Rome were regarded as producing bad wine, but Martial, who condemned the stuff, may have had some prejudice about it. We are well aware that Etruria—now Tuscany —is producing some of the most agreeable of Italian wines today. A fine red Chianti, enjoyed in Italy rather than in a country to which it is exported, has high merit; and a white Orvieto of a good year can take its place among the finest wines of Europe. Long before Martial decried the wines of Etruria, the Etruscans themselves in the days of their glory must have made fine drink after the manner of the Greeks and the inhabitants of Anatolia whence this remarkable people had come to settle in Italy.

Undoubtedly they were a drinking—often it seems a drunken —lot. And this applied to their women as much as to their men.

Timaeus of Syracuse and Theopompus of Chios, both fourth-century writers, were quoted by Athenaeus on the subject of Etruscan habits. The Tuscans were culturally linked both to the Lydians and to the Ionians, wearing Ionic garb and importing many luxuries from Asia Minor. The words of Athenaeus, indeed, give an impression of liberty slopping over into licence:

Among the Etruscans, who had become extravagantly luxurious, Timaeus in his first book relates that naked slave-girls wait on the men.

And Theopompus in the forty-third book of his Histories says that it is a custom among Etruscans to share their women in common; the women take very great care of their bodies and often exercise naked even with men, sometimes also with one another; for it is no disgrace for women to appear naked. And they dine, not with their own husbands but with any men who happen to be present, and they pledge in their cups any whom they wish. They are also terribly bibulous, and are remarkably beautiful. The Etruscans rear all the children that are born, not knowing who is the father in any single case. These in turn pursue the same mode of life as those who have brought them up, having drinking parties often, and consorting with all the women. It is no disgrace for Etruscans to be seen doing anything in the open, or even having anything done to them; for this, too, is a custom of the country.[5]

The grim thing for a moralist in all this is that apparently the Etruscans were none the worse for it. They remained formidable and were long feared alike by Roman, Latin and Italiote Greek. Not only could the Etruscan lords and ladies surpass any of the reported orgies of the Italian Renaissance, but it would appear that one of Nero's parties was probably very much tamer than a Tuscan banquet. Meanwhile, the beauty of the women of Tuscany and the excellence of Tuscan wine can still be remarked today.[6]

Beyond Etruria there must have been plenty of good wines in the north of Italy; and the beginning of viticulture in Gaul, including the valleys of Rhone and Rhine, was early. With the foundation of Marseilles, about 600 B.C. by Greeks from Ionia, Hellenic influence spread quickly into the southern part of Gaul—that country which we now call France—and it assuredly brought with it the amenities of wine and olive oil, so essential to civilisation. From some such small beginnings there sprang the ancestors of those great wines—and of spirits distilled from the grape—

[5] Athenaeus, *The Sages at Dinner*, 517 d. The reader interested in the topic of orgies will find yet further curious information in the passages immediately following the one I have translated. There is a good translation in the Loeb Classical Library *Athenaeus*.

[6] Seltman, *Women in Antiquity* (Pan), pp. 76 f.

which today still command the respect of all civilised men and women. Had Greeks never established in Provence their famous colonies, Massalia, Nicea, Antipolis, and lesser settlements we might have classed the people of France as mere beer or cider drinkers. But as things are when we mention, with a touch of reverence, the great Champagnes, Clarets, Burgundies, wines of the Saone and Rhone, Hocks and Moselles, and many another, we may say "all this was started by certain vivid and adventurous Greeks". Whether or no some of them, at some time before the Graeco-Roman empire fell to pieces, ever discovered—empirically of course—how to distil spirit from grapes is uncertain. But those things we vaguely describe as "brandy", or more carefully as "*fine*", "*cognac*", "*armagnac*", are actually derivatives still bequeathed by Dionysos-Bacchos to the human race.

For myself I enjoyed some twenty-five years ago a most interesting experience of a very special wine liqueur. Staying with the head of one of the famous families which produce champagne, the topic of the taste and survival of ancient drinks was discussed among us. My host sent for his valet in charge of the cellar-book, and discovered that he still had two bottles of a brandy made under unusual and experimental circumstances by an ancestor and bottled in 1786, three years before the French Revolution began. The ancestor had made a brandy in the manner then customary in the regions of Cognac and Armagnac—but in Champagne, and with champagne grapes. An old green bottle was opened, and we drank out of small gold liqueur-glasses. Extreme delicacy of taste was the main impression. It was soft, dry, and less alcoholic even than old "Napoleon" brandy. It seems worth recording this experience because it must confirm the general opinion that if ever any Greek or Roman wine-jar were opened the liquid within would have long lost any trace of vinous essence.

*Chapter Ten*

❖❖❖❖❖❖❖❖❖❖❖❖❖❖❖❖❖❖❖❖❖❖❖❖❖❖❖❖❖❖❖❖❖❖❖❖❖❖❖❖❖❖❖

# DE BACCHANALIBUS

❖❖❖❖❖❖❖❖❖❖❖❖❖❖❖❖❖❖❖❖❖❖❖❖❖❖❖❖❖❖❖❖❖❖❖❖❖❖❖❖❖❖❖

ROME which grew into so mighty an empire began its life in a very small way. A little Latin village of shepherds perched on a hill beside the only ford across the Tiber, and closer to that river's mouth than any of the other settlements. Nearby an Oscan Sabine settlement, which first seemed an enemy, presently merged with the Latins and the town grew to be a city set upon seven hills. Then Rome, which the Etruscans called *Ruma*, became during the sixth century B.C. the centre of an Etruscan kingdom which introduced Tuscan ideas of art and religion. Though the last king was expelled, according to tradition, about 509 B.C. the foreign gods did not depart, and the Romans knew about a wine-god, resembling the Greek Dionysos, to whom the Etruscans gave the extraordinary name of *Fufluns*. Not until 186 B.C. was the Roman administration to encounter a terrifying form of the real Greek Dionysos-Bacchos. The whole episode so impressed the historian Livy that, when he gave an account of these events in the reign of Augustus many years later he went into considerable and interesting details,[1] and his History relating the happenings in the year 186 B.C. opens in sinister mood.

The following year diverted Spurius Postumius Albinus and Quintus Marcius Philippus, from the care of armies, and wars, and

[1] The passages are translated from Livy, Book 39, Chapters 8 and following.

provinces, to the punishing of an intestine conspiracy. The making inquisition concerning clandestine meetings was decreed to both the consuls. A Greek of mean condition came first into Etruria, not with one of the many trades which his nation, of all others the most skilful in the cultivation of the mind and body, has introduced among us, but a low operator in sacrifices, and a soothsayer; nor was he one who, by open religious rites, and by publicly professing his calling and teaching, imbued the minds of his followers with terror, but a priest of secret and nocturnal rites. These mysterious rites were, at first, imparted to a few, but afterwards communicated to great numbers, both men and women. To their religious performances were added the pleasures of wine and feasting, to allure a greater number of proselytes. When wine, lascivious discourse, night, and the intercourse of the sexes had extinguished every sentiment of modesty, then debaucheries of every kind began to be practised, as every person found at hand that sort of enjoyment to which he was disposed by the passion predominant in his nature. Nor were they confined to one species of vice—the promiscuous intercourse of free-born men and women; but from this store-house of villainy proceeded false witnesses, counterfeit seals, false evidences, and pretended discoveries. From the same place, too, proceeded poison and secret murders, so that in some cases, even the bodies could not be found for burial. Many of their audacious deeds were brought about by treachery, but most of them by force; it served to conceal the violence, that, on account of the loud shouting, and the noise of drums and cymbals, none of the cries uttered by the persons suffering violation or murder could be heard abroad.

The infection of this mischief, like that from the contagion of disease, spread from Etruria to Rome, where, the size of the city affording greater room for such evils, and more means of concealment, cloaked it at first; but information of it was at length brought to the consul, Postumius, principally in the following manner. Publius Aebutius, whose father had held equestrian rank in the army, was left an orphan, and his guardians dying, he was educated under the eye of his mother Duronia, and his stepfather Titus Sempronius Rutilus. Duronia was entirely devoted to her husband; and Sempronius, having managed the guardianship in such a manner that he could not give an account of the property, wishing that his ward should be either made away with or bound to compliance with his will by some strong tie, thought that the Bacchanalian rites were the only way to effect the ruin of the youth. His mother told the young man, that, during his sickness, she had made a vow for him, that if he should recover, she would initiate him among the Bacchanalians; and that being, through the kindness of the gods, bound by this vow, she wished now to fulfil it; that it was necessary he should preserve chastity for ten days, and on the tenth after he should have supped and washed himself she would conduct him into the place of worship. There was a freedwoman called Hispala Fecenia, a noted courtesan, but deserving of a better lot than the mode of life to which she had been accustomed when very young, as a slave, and by which she had maintained herself since her manumission. As they lived in the same neighbourhood, a liaison subsisted between her and Aebutius, which was far from being injurious either to the young man's character or property; for he had been loved and wooed by her unsolicited; and as his friends supplied his wants illiberally, he was supported by the generosity of this woman; nay, to such a length did she go under the influence of her affection, that, on the death of her patron, because she was under the protection of no one, having petitioned the tribunes and praetors for a guardian, when she was making her will, she constituted Aebutius her sole heir.

As such pledges of mutual love existed, and as neither kept any thing secret from the other, the young man, jokingly, bid her not be surprised if he separated himself from her for a few nights; as, on account of a religious duty, to discharge a vow made for his health, he intended to be initiated among the Bacchanalians. On hearing this, the woman, greatly alarmed, cried out, "May the Gods will more favourably!" affirming that it would be better, both for him and her, to lose their lives than that he should do such a thing: she then imprecated curses, vengeance, and destruction, on the head of those who advised him to such a step. The young man, surprised both at her expressions and at the violence of her alarm, bid her refrain from curses, for it was his mother who ordered him to do so, with the approbation of his stepfather. "Then," said she, "your stepfather (for perhaps it is not allowable to censure your mother) is in haste to destroy, by that act, your chastity, your character, your hopes, and your life." To him, now surprised by such language, and inquiring what was the matter, she said (after imploring the favour and pardon of the gods and goddesses, if, compelled by her regard for him she disclosed what ought not to be revealed) that when in service, she had gone into that place of worship, as an attendant on her mistress; but that, since she had obtained her liberty, she had never once gone near it: that she knew it to be the receptacle of all kinds of debaucheries; that it was well known that, for two years past, no one older than twenty had been initiated there.

Gradually the revelations of these two were made known to one of the consuls, Postumius Albinus, who set all the details before the Senate.

Great consternation seized the senators; not only on the public account, lest such conspiracies and nightly meetings might be productive of secret treachery and mischief, but also on account of their own particular families, lest some of their relations might be involved in this infamous affair. The Senate voted, however, that thanks should be given to the consul because he had investigated the matter with singular diligence, and without exciting any alarm. They then committed to the consul the holding of an inquiry, out of the common course, concerning the Bacchanals and their nocturnal orgies. They ordered them to take care that the informers, Aebutius and Fecenia, should suffer no injury on that account; and to invite other informers by offering rewards. They ordered that the officials in those rites, whether men or women, should be sought out, not only at Rome, but also throughout all market towns and places of assembly, and that they be handed over to the power of the consuls; and also that proclamation should be made in the city of Rome, and published through all Italy, that no persons initiated into Bacchanalian rites should presume to come together or assemble on account of those rites, or to perform any kind of worship; and above all, that search should be made for those who had assembled or conspired for personal abuse or for any other flagitious practices.

During the night, which succeeded the day in which the affair was made public, great numbers, attempting to fly, were seized, and brought back by the triumvirs, who had posted guards at all the gates; and information was lodged against many, some of whom, both men and women, put themselves to death. Above seven thousand men and women are said to have taken the oath of the association.

Those who, as it appeared, had been only initiated, and had repeated after the priest, and in the most solemn form, the prescribed imprecations, in which the accursed conspiracy for the perpetration of every crime and lust was contained, but who had not themselves committed, or compelled others to commit, any of those acts to which they were bound by the oath—all such they left in prison. But those who had forcibly committed personal defilements or murders, or were stained with the guilt of false evidence, counterfeit seals, forged wills, or other frauds, all these they punished with death. A greater number were executed than thrown into prison; indeed, the multitude of men and women who suffered in both ways, was very considerable. The consuls delivered the women, who were condemned, to their relations, or to those under whose guardianship they were, that they might inflict the punishment in private; but if there did not appear any proper person of the kind to execute the sentence, the punishment was inflicted in public. A charge was then given to demolish all places where the Bacchanalians had held their meetings; first, in Rome, and then throughout all Italy; excepting those wherein should be found some ancient altar, or consecrated statue. With regard to the future, the senate passed a Decree, that no Bacchanalian rites should be celebrated in Rome or in Italy:

This celebrated Decree, known as the *Senatus Consultum de Bacchanalibus*, was set up, not only in Rome, but throughout Italy, and one of these inscriptions survives[2] more accurate than the often retranscribed text of Livy; for the bronze tablet found in Calabria, and now in Vienna, is that rare treasure, a contemporary original. The main text runs as follows:

In the matter of Bacchanalia, the senate decrees that the allies shall make proclamation as follows: "Let none of their number attempt to hold a Bacchanal: If there be any who persuade themselves that it is needful to hold a Bacchanal, let them come to the praetor urbanus, at Rome, and on this matter, when their appeal has been heard, let our Senate decide, provided that no fewer than 100 Senators have been present when the case was in debate. No Roman citizen nor citizen with Latin rights nor with allied right shall become a 'Bacchos' save with the permission of the praetor urbanus."

What an astonishing episode it all was! For it was religious persecution on the grand scale, such as the Mediterranean has scarcely seen apart from what the Israelites did to their polytheistic neighbours when strong enough to do so. The ancient

---

[2] In Vienna (I.L. i², 581, x, 104; Dessau 18; Diehl 5; Shuckburgh, p. 54) and is to be compared with Livy's version in Book 39, Chapter 18.

world from Mesopotamia to Spain too often indulged in political persecution combined with the enslavement of men and women, but interference with other peoples' beliefs was rare indeed before the reign of Nero. The slaughter and incarceration of over 7000 men and women on the evidence of informers who must grossly have exaggerated aspects of Bacchic worship is a matter for remark by any historian; and one may draw a parallel between the savage, but open-air activities of Euripides' Bacchantes3 and the underground "goings-on" of the second-century Romans. When, however, it was all over, for the time being, the God of wine despised and rejected of men, the supposed guilty persons executed, the women—wives or daughters—bound and handed over to husbands or fathers whose duty and privilege it was to kill them4, hundreds flung into dark and unspeakable dungeons; when it was all over the Senate suddenly cooled down and promulgated the astonishing Decree which has just been cited.

In the second century B.C. there were already many influential members of the Senate who, as philhellenes, spoke Greek, had cultivated Greek friends and were familiar with Greek literature. Men like the great Scipio and Flamininus must have read the Euripidean *Bacchai* and known of the legendary fate of Pentheus—that awful warning not to oppose a God. They must have known enough about Greek history to have learnt how Peisistratus and other famous tyrants canalised the worship of Dionysos into the theatre and the rhythmical wanderings of thyiads and maenads. They had their own strong influence in the Roman senate among the less cultivated men who, none the less, were legatistic to the core. Human nature was comprehended, together with the principle that—except among primitive tribes—any absolute "thou shalt not" breeds resentment followed by rebellion. Therefore the Senate in this most noteworthy of Decrees took a line that can be paraphrased as follows: "be Bacchanalian if you really want to after having obtained a signed Government

3 See above, pp. 55 ff.
4 See my *Women in Antiquity* (Pan), p. 137; (Thames and Hudson), pp. 170 ff.

permit authorising your orgiastic behaviour the said permit to
have first affixed to it the official stamp of the Chief of the Metro-
politan Police Force".

Who would wish to indulge in a legalised, police-inspected
Dionysiac frenzy? And yet the god's cultus had not quite been
exiled nor anathematised.

Wine was not forbidden and the Roman Republic did not
become the first Prohibitionist community. That phenomenon
was almost unknown in antiquity, although we must not forget
one little group dedicated, among other things, to an hostility to
wine. These were the so-called Rechabites, the name Rechab
meaning "a company of Riders", who traced their customs to
Jehonadab, and are mentioned as early as the time of Jehu, about
840 B.C. and are highly commended by Jeremiah for their implicit
obedience to ancestral precepts.5 These people were horse- and
cattle-owning nomads of ancient Hebrew stock who refused to
take part in the pleasures and dubious religious practices of city
life in the land of Canaan. They themselves recounted their com-
mandments to Jeremiah in the following words:

We will drink no wine: for Jehonadab the son of Rechab
our father commanded us, saying, Ye shall drink no wine,
neither ye, nor your sons, for ever: neither shall ye build house,
nor sow seed, nor plant vineyard, nor have any: but all your
days ye shall dwell in tents, that ye may live many days in the
land wherein ye sojourn.

Many centuries later there arose in the Near East another to
forbid the use of wine: The Prophet himself. Edward Gibbon6
as always has the delightful phrase and the appealing comment.

The interdiction of wine was confirmed by his example; his hunger
was appeased with a sparing allowance of barley bread; he delighted
in the taste of milk and honey; but his ordinary food consisted of dates
and water. Perfumes and women were the two sensual enjoyments

5 II *Kings* x, 15, 23; *Jeremiah* xxxv; H. St J. Hart, *A Foreword to the Old
Testament*, pp. 43 f.
6 *Decline and Fall of the Roman Empire*, Vol. V (World's Classics),
pp. 446 f.

which his nature required and his religion did not forbid; and Mahomet affirmed that the fervour of his devotion was increased by these innocent pleasures. But in his private conduct Mahomet indulged the appetites of a man and abused the claims of a prophet. A special revelation dispensed him from the laws which he had imposed on his nation; the female sex, without reserve, was abandoned to his desires; and this singular prerogative excited the envy, rather than the scandal, the veneration, rather than the envy, of the devout Musulmans. If we remember the seven hundred wives and three hundred concubines of the wise Solomon, we shall applaud the modesty of the Arabian, who espoused no more than seventeen or fifteen wives. In the largest indulgence of polygamy, the founder of a religion and empire might aspire to multiply the chances of a numerous posterity and a lineal succession. The hopes of Mahomet were fatally disappointed. The virgin Ayesha, and his ten widows of mature age and approved fertility, were barren in his potent embraces.

The frivolous historian may be tempted to suggest that had the Prophet shown some deference to Dionysos he might have begotten sons. Another point of interest is to observe that the founders of Salt Lake City and the State of Utah were dedicated like the early Moslems to the propositions of polygamy and total abstinence from wine.

That the virtual suppression of Bacchic cult in second-century Roman Italy was accompanied by martyrdom is not in doubt. Probably the worship benefited by a persecution which began in time to increase the number of fresh converts; for one observes the same thing happening within the frame of Christianity much later.

Livy, who had access to so much information, gives the figure of the victims at about 7000 people, which seems to be a far higher figure than what has been estimated for the last great Imperial persecution under Diocletian. Professional English and American martyrologists have quoted figures up to 40,000, but French Catholic scholars will have none of this. One writer, Father Delahaye,[7] reduced the martyrs to a small number, while another[8]

7 *Legends of the Saints* (1922).
8 Monsignor Duchesne: *History of the Christian Church*, 3 vols. (1904-29).

recognises an even smaller collection of little more than a score. Naturally the nonsensical assemblages of the 11,000 virgin martyrs with St Ursula, and of St Pappus with his 24,000 companions have to be scrapped.9 It may well be that the Republican treatment of Bacchanals surpassed in persecution anything that the Empire performed; for it is hard to believe that more than a few hundred Christians were killed in two and a half centuries.

Wine, however, continued ever more and more in use among the ancient Romans. They and the other central Italian peoples had learnt the technique of vintage, either from the Etruscans who had brought the methods with them from Anatolia, or from the South Italian Greeks who knew how to grow grapes and make wine after the manner of the Greeks in their original homelands. One method was certainly just like another, and it has been briefly described above in Chapter 5. Accordingly we have only to mention those Latin words which correspond to the Greek terminology. Fresh grape-juice, *gleukos* in Greek is *mustum* in Latin; grape-jelly, Greek, *hepsema*, Latin, *defrutum* (whence Italian musto cotto, otherwise sapa, French sabe); retsina, Greek *oinos retinites* is in Latin *resinatum*. And the vessels to contain the wine known as *pithoi* and *amphorai* in Greek had, in Latin, the names *dolia* and *lagoenae*. When wine was inadequately preserved—no unusual thing in ancient Italy—it turned to vinegar, and when vinegar exposed to the air lost its acidity it became completely insipid. The Latin name for such stuff was *vappa*, and the Romans used that word figuratively for a worthless blockhead. This name for a good-for-nothing still persists in Neapolitan dialect and appears as "woppo". Applied years ago as a term of abuse by one New York Italian about another, it entered into American slang, and so the word "wop" became the standard appellation for any inferior Italian today.

The main ancient Latin writers to contribute information on wine were Cato, of the second century B.C., and Varro, who

9 Father F. G. Holweck, *A Biographical Dictionary of the Saints* (St Louis, 1924), reduces these two collections to eleven and to twenty-three persons. Perhaps an overestimate.

flourished about 50 B.C. To these sources one may add the Twelfth Book of Columella, Varro's contemporary, and the Fourteenth with part of the Twenty-third Books of the *Natural History* by the elder Pliny produced in the mid-first century of our era. There is something too in the Second Book of Virgil's *Georgics*, and allusions abound in the works of other poets.

It is well known that all the most excellent Italian wines, with few exceptions, were derived from Latium and Campania, and for the most part grew within a short distance of the sea. "The whole of these places", says Strabo, when describing this coast, "yield excellent wine; among the most celebrated are the Caecuban, the Fundanian, the Setinian and also the Falernian, the Alban, and the Statinian." In the first rank, then, one should place the Setinum, which fairly deserves the title of Imperial, since it was the chosen beverage of Augustus and most of his court. It grew upon the hills of Setia, above Forum Appii, looking down upon the Pomptine marshes. Before the age of Augustus the Caecubum was the most prized of all. It grew in the poplar swamps bordering on the gulf of Amyclae, close to Fundi. In the time of Pliny its reputation was entirely gone, partly in consequence of the carelessness of the cultivators, and partly because its proper soil, originally a very limited space, had been cut up by the canal of Nero extending from Baiae to Ostia. The second rank was occupied by the Falernum, of which the Faustianum was the most choice variety, having gained its character from the care and skill exercised in the cultivation of the vines; but when Pliny wrote it was beginning to fall in public estimation, because the wine-growers had become more interested in quantity than in quality. The Falernus ager, concerning the precise limits of which there have been controversies, commenced at the Pons Campanus, on the left hand of those journeying towards the Urbana Colonia of Sulla; the Faustianus ager at a village about six miles from Sinuessa. Falernian became fit for drinking in ten years, and might be used when twenty years old, but when kept longer might cause a headache, and overtax the nervous system; in other words produce a hangover. Pliny distinguishes three kinds, the rough, the sweet and the thin; Galen two only, the rough and the sweetish. The ordinary appearance of Falernian seems to be determined by a passage in Pliny in which we are informed that the finest amber was named Falerna. In the third rank was the Albanum, from the Mons Albanus of various kinds, very sweet, sweetish, rough and sharp; it was invigorating and in perfection after being kept for fifteen years. Here one may compare the Surrentinum, from Sorrento on the promontory forming the southern horn of the bay of Naples, which was not drinkable until it had been kept for five and twenty years; for, lacking body and being very dry it required a long time to mature, but it was recommended to convalescents, on account of its thinness and wholesomeness. Galen, however, was of opinion that it agreed only with people who were accustomed to use it constantly. Tiberius declared that the doctors had conspired to dignify what was no more than generous vinegar; while his successor, Caligula, mocked it as *nobilis vappa*. Of equal reputation were the Massicum, from the hills which formed the boundary between Latium and Campania—although somewhat harsh, as would seem, from the precautions recommended by the epicure in Horace—and the Gauranum, from the ridge above Baiae and Puteoli, produced in small quantity, but of very high quality, full-bodied and thick. In the same class are to be included the Calenum from Cales, and the Fundanum from Fundi. Both had formerly held a higher place, " but vineyards," Pliny remarks, "like States, have their periods of rise, of glory, and of fall". The Calenum was light and better for the stomach than Falernian; the Fundanum was full-bodied and nourishing, but apt to upset both stomach and head and so not suitable as a table wine.

Medical authorities, like Galen, were given to commending the use of wine in moderation to their patients, and this was natural, since no elaborate system of drugs, compounded medicines and tonics had been evolved, and any Greek and Roman science of chemistry was elementary. Vitamins and calories had not been discovered. Nowadays the experts may declare that things like ham and eggs, or fish and chips contain each dish, 250 calories,

that meat pie jumps up to 350 calories, and that a strange con-
coction called "fruit sundae" tops the bill with 800 calories. At the
opposite end of the scale the experts place Brandy with 100
calories, Champagne with 90, Sherry with 80, and Burgundy with
75; while Dionysos himself, the bunch of grapes, is allowed no
more than 50 calories.

But if *in vino veritas* is acceptable then so, surely, is *in vino
sanitas*. Some have been known to drink a Health in spirits, in
beer, in tomato juice, and, most lamentably, even in water. None
of these things are proper for a Health.

Therefore when we rise from table to the toast "Gentlemen,
The Queen!" let it be drunk in wine.

*Chapter Eleven*

❖❖❖❖❖❖❖❖❖❖❖❖❖❖❖❖❖❖❖❖❖❖❖❖❖❖❖❖❖❖❖❖❖❖❖

# ROMAN BANQUET

❖❖❖❖❖❖❖❖❖❖❖❖❖❖❖❖❖❖❖❖❖❖❖❖❖❖❖❖❖❖❖❖❖❖❖

QUITE apart from the Greek Dionysos Bromios Bacchos, and apart from the Etruscan Fufluns, the Romans and Latins had got a god in charge of grapes and wine whom they called Liber. They invented for him a wife called Libera, who, in their somewhat misty religious mythology, became identified either with Ceres—a corn goddess—easily equated with the Greek Demeter, or with her daughter Proserpina who was a kind of reduplication of her mother. Liber, sometimes called Liber Pater, and his wife seem to have been the deities of wine and corn. It is not possible to know whether this association of gods came to Rome and Latium from Anatolia by way of Etruria, or whether it was an independent concept built up within the vague and illogical framework of early Roman religion. These deities might have faded out altogether, Bacchus replacing them, but for the fact that Augustus, who strove to revive antique Republican piety, refounded a temple for Liber, Libera and Ceres, and his successor Tiberius dedicated it. Yet despite this archaising attempt it was Bacchus who prevailed throughout the Empire.

Roman Africa produced some wine of quality just as Algeria does today—good but not remarkable. But even in late Republican times Gaul was beginning to excel, and, as the wines of Italy declined from neglect or from over-production, those of the land that was to become France grew in virtue. From small beginnings in cities of the Greek fringe on the south coast and among Roman connoisseurs administering the earliest of all Roman provinces—Provence, there were gradually developed through centuries all the finest wines in the world.

Up the Rhône there are the sensational wines like Hermitage, Côte-Rôtie and Tavel; over to Burgundy to find rich, full-bodied wines like Beaujolais, Mâcon, Nuits and Beaune with their white sisters, Chablis, Meursault, Montrachet and fine flinty Pouilly Fuissé. Westward on the Loire and Cher are Rosé d'Anjou, Saumur and dainty Vouvray, and further west the great clarets of Bordeaux: Saint Emilion, Médoc, Pomerol and the white Sauternes and Graves. The Moselle of Alsace achieved early fame and the names Riesling, Traminer, Sylvaner have a Gallo-Germanic ring. Last, but not least, one must recall the products centred round Rheims and Epernay. A generation ago there were wine-drinkers who affected a scorn of Champagne. The pose has now flopped, for these sparkling wines have about them something of divinity. They are right for every occasion and for every kind of meal. Asklepios would have ordered Champagne for his patients, Dionysos would have cried out "This, at last, is the essential ME!" The heroes of Homer, the elegant Athenians, the Roman poets, even the Alexandrians down to Athenaeus and his Gastronomers would have purred with pleasure; but ice or snow is a requisite. Indeed one of its greatest virtues is that most men and women can take so much with so little ill effect. It is the great French miracle, quite unknown to the ancient world. But how they would have loved it!

Wines should always be named after the regions where they grow. Emotional labels like Lacrima Christi at Naples and Liebfraumilch on the Rhine carry a tang of advertising about them; but clever salesmanship is no evidence for the virtues of a wine. What is noteworthy is that the supreme wines of France and the excellent vintages of other European regions all spring from the ancient fruit that Dionysos-Bacchos gave to Greece and Italy.

Good wine, if not superb wine, can be made in regions further north than those provinces which have received brief mention. The Curé of Montmartre—once a village on the Roman Hill of Mars north of Paris but now absorbed in the capital—has his own trim vineyard on a favourable and sheltered slope of the hill, and it provides him with a pleasant annual supply of white wine to be laid down. In southern England there are venturesome men today who, having learnt the job, are growing their own grapes out of doors and making their own small cellars, strictly for personal consumption, since Customs and Excise would pursue them relentlessly were they to trade. For tourists the best-known vine is the one at Hampton Court which bears grapes and is alleged to have come from stock brought over by the Romans though planted, of course, by Wolsey. Had the English not been such devotees of ale that famous man might have started a new fashion and from his vine there might have spread a famous Hampton Court *cru* known as "Château Neuf du Cardinal".

Be that as it may, when Britain became a province of the Empire the Romans brought the grape with them, and it grew as successfully in Kent, Sussex, Hampshire, the Isle of Wight and Dorset, as it does today on Montmartre.

Rich Romans of the first century of our era had as large and varied a repertoire of wines to draw upon as the wealthy have today, and they went for the "right" names and for the famous years when they could obtain them. Trimalchio, in that most fantastic of ancient stories, the *Satyricon* of Petronius, served his guests with the most expensive wine obtainable.

"Falernian of Opimius's vintage,[1] one hundred years in bottle," and as we were reading the labels Trimalchio clapped his hands and cried "alas that wine lives longer than wretched man! So let us wet our whistles, for wine is life!"

But the Banquet of Trimalchio is deserving of further study, if only for its absurd contrast with an Athenian symposium of the

[1] Opimius was consul in 121 B.C.

fifth century B.C. such as was described in our first chapter.
Tacitus in the sixteenth book of his *Annals* gave a brief characteri-
sation of Petronius, author of the celebrated *Satyricon*.[2]

Gaius Petronius spent his days sleeping, his nights working and
enjoying himself. Others achieved fame by energy, Petronius by lazi-
ness. Yet he was not like others who waste their resources, regarded as
dissipated or extravagant, but as a refined voluptuary. People liked the
apparent freshness of his unconventional and unselfconscious sayings
and doings. He had been admitted into the small circle of Nero's
intimates, as Arbiter of Taste: to the blasé emperor, smartness and elegance were restricted to what Petronius had approved. So Tigellinus,
loathing him as a rival and expert hedonist, denounced him. This
appealed to the emperor's outstanding passion—his cruelty. A slave
was bribed to incriminate Petronius. No defence was heard. Indeed,
most of his household were under arrest.

The emperor happened to be in Campania. Petronius too had
reached Cumae; there he was detained. Delay, with its hopes and fears,
he refused to endure. He severed his veins. Then, having them bound
up again when the fancy took him, he talked with his friends—but not
seriously, or so as to gain a name for fortitude. And he listened to them
reciting, not discourses about the immortality of the soul or philosophy, but light lyrics and frivolous poems. He appeared at dinner, and
dozed, so that his death, if compulsory, might look natural.

In his famous work with its loose construction nothing
mattered to Petronius except good writing. There is no moral to
the book but only a presentation of things as they appeared to an
elegant philanderer in Roman Italy. The name of his work
*Satyricon* just means a medley, and what survives of it ambles
along without plan. Yet it is a novel—the first in the Latin language and surpassingly brilliant. Action centres round a group of
three, Encolpius, who tells the story, his brother Ascyltos, and a
catamite named Giton who trails around with them. And it is
when these three are introduced by the kindness of a teacher
of rhetoric, calling himself Agamemnon, to the *nouveau-riche*

[2] Quotation is from the translation by Michael Grant, *Tacitus on Imperial
Rome* (Penguin Classics), 1956.

plutocrat Trimalchio that the best surviving chapters of the novel are developed, for the three are invited as guests to his party. Here is a group of characters and a startling picture of life in an Italian provincial town.

The pulsating energy of greed is felt in it everywhere. Men become millionaires with American rapidity, and enjoy that condition as hazardously in Cumae as in Wall Street. The shoulders of one who wallows in Trimalchio's cushions are still sore with carrying firewood for sale; another, perhaps the first undertaker who made a fortune out of extravagant funerals, a gourmet and spendthrift, sits there composing lies to baffle his hungry creditors. Trimalchio towers above them by reason of his more stable fortunes and his colossal impudence. He can afford to delegate the conduct of his business, to grow a little negligent, even—for his accounts are six months in arrear—to care for the life of the spirit.3

He boasts the possession of two libraries, but his comical muddleheadedness is evidence that he is almost illiterate; and his attempts at expounding Greek mythology could only be equalled by a half-wit Irish peasant trying to explain the doctrines of the Catholic Church. Only one of the guests in the novel, named Ganymede, shows up the darkness against which the prosperity of Trimalchio and his cronies is seen. While the millionaire has his bath, his fine sanitation, his large company of obsequious servants, really poor and destitute creatures are dying in the streets of Cumae; yet these newly-rich monsters pretend that the problem is simply not there.

Fortunata is the wife of Trimalchio. He bought her—a slave prostitute—in the open market. She is now a "lady" whom hard experience has taught how to manage stupid and brutish men like her husband. One other woman is present at this fantastic dinner party, Scintilla—wife of Habinnas, a monumental mason—and she drinks more and behaves worse than her friend Fortunata. Enough has been said to outline the cynical, witty accounts of this shocking party and one feels sure that Petronius himself must

3 See Michael Heseltine, *Petronius* (Loeb Classical Library), pp. xi f.

have been a guest at more than one such feast. It could not have grown, all of it, out of his imagination.

Since, in our first chapter, considerable excerpts were taken from Xenophon's elegant Symposium, it is only fair to extract a few details from the Banquet of Trimalchio, and to appreciate the contrast. Numerous long passages have been omitted.

"We reclined on the couches while Alexandrian boys poured water cooled with snow over our hands. Others followed and knelt down at our feet, and proceeded with great skill to pare our corns. Even this unpleasant duty did not silence them but they kept singing at their work. I wanted to find out whether the whole household sang, so I asked for a drink. Promptly a boy repeated my order in a high chanting voice. They all did the same if they were asked to hand anything. It was more like an actor's dance than a gentleman's dining-room. But some tasty morsels were brought in; for every one had now sat down except Trimalchio, who had the first place reserved for him in the new style. The *hors d'œuvres* were served; hot sausages on a silver grill, and under the grill damsons and pomegranate seeds.

"We were enjoying these delicacies, when Trimalchio himself was conducted in to the sound of music, propped on the tiniest of pillows. A laugh escaped the unwary. His shaven head peered out of a scarlet cloak, and over the heavy clothes on his neck he had put on a scarf with a broad stripe and fringes hanging from it all round. On the little finger of his left hand he had an enormous gilt ring which appeared to me to be entirely gold, but was really set all round with iron cut out in little stars. Not content with this display of wealth, he bared his right arm, where a golden bracelet shone, and an ivory bangle clasped with a plate of bright metal. Then he said, as he picked his teeth with a silver quill, 'My friends, it was not convenient for me to come to dinner yet, but I gave up all my own pleasure; I did not like to stay away any longer and keep you waiting.' Trimalchio now asked for the same dishes, and in a loud voice invited any of us to take a second *aperitif*. Then two hairy Ethiopians with little wine-skins, just like the men who scatter sand in an amphitheatre, came in and gave us wine to wash our hands in, for no one offered us water. 'Now', said Trimalchio, 'let us have dinner. This is sauce for the dinner.' As he spoke, four dancers ran up in time with the music and took off the top part of the dish. Then we saw in the well of it fat fowls and sows' bellies, and in the middle a hare got up with wings to look like Pegasus. Four figures of Marsyas at the corners of the dish also caught the eye; they let a spiced sauce run from their wine-skins over the fishes, which swam about in a kind of tide-race. We all took up the clapping which the slaves started, and attacked these delicacies with hearty laughter. Trimalchio was delighted with the trick he had played us, and said, 'Now, Carver!' The man came up at once, and making flourishes in time with the music pulled the dish to pieces, you would have said that a hero in a chariot was fighting to the accompaniment of a water-organ. Still Trimalchio kept on in a soft voice, 'Oh, Carver, Carver.' I thought this word over and over again must be part of a joke, and I made bold to ask the man who sat next me this very question. He had seen performances of this kind more often. 'You see the fellow who is carving his way through the meat? Well, his name is Carver. So whenever Trimalchio says the word, you have his name, and he has his orders.'

"I was now unable to eat any more, so I turned to my neighbour to get as much news as possible. I began to seek for far-fetched stories, and to inquire who the woman was who kept running about this way and that. 'She's Trimalchio's wife, Fortunata,' he said, 'and she counts her money by the bushel. And what was she a little while ago? You will pardon me if I say that you would not have taken a piece of bread from her hand. Now without why or how she's queen of Heaven, and Trimalchio's all in all. If she told him it was dark at high noon, he'd believe it. He is so enormously rich that he does not know himself what he has; but this bitch has a plan for everything, even where you'd not expect it. She's temperate, sober, prudent, but has a nasty tongue, and she henpecks him on his own sofa. Whom she likes, he likes; whom she dislikes, he dislikes. Trimalchio has estates wherever a kite can fly in a day, is millionaire of millionaires. There is more plate lying in his steward's room than other people have in their whole fortunes. So high is his felicity.

"'But do not look down on the other freedmen who are his friends. They are very juicy people. That one you see lying on the bottom couch has his eight hundred thousand. He was quite a nobody. A little time ago he was carrying loads of wood on his back. People do say—I know nothing, but I have heard—that he pulled off a goblin's cap and found a fairy hoard. If gods make presents I'm jealous of nobody. Still, he shows the marks of his master's fingers, and has a fine opinion of himself. So he has just put up a notice on his hovel: "This attic, property of Caius Pompeius Diogenes, to let from the 1st of July, the owner having purchased a house." That person there too who is lying in the freedman's place is well pleased with himself. I don't blame him. He had his million in his hands, but he has had a bad shaking, I believe he cannot call his hair his own. No fault, by Hercules, of his; there's no better fellow alive; but it is the damned freedmen who have pocketed everything. You know how it is: the company's pot goes off the boil, and the moment business takes a bad turn your friends desert you. You see him in this state: and what a fine trade he drove! He was an undertaker. He used to dine like a prince: hams boiled in cloths, wonderful sweets, game; yes and chefs and pastry-cooks! There used to be more wine spilt under the table than many a man has in his cellars. He was a fairy prince, not a mortal. When his business was failing, and he was afraid his creditors might guess that he was going bankrupt, he advertised a sale in this fashion: "Caius Julius Proculus will offer for sale some articles for which he has no further use."'

"Trimalchio interrupted these delightful tales; the meat had now been removed, and the cheerful company began to turn their attention to the wine, and to general conversation. He lay back on his couch and said, 'Now you must make this wine go down pleasantly.'

"As we were speaking, a beautiful boy with vine-leaves and ivy in his hair brought round grapes in a little basket, impersonating Bromios in ecstasy, Bacchus full of wine, Bacchus dreaming, and rendering his master's verses in a most shrill voice. Trimalchio turned round at the noise and said, 'Dionysus, rise and be free.' Then Trimalchio went on: 'I am sure you will agree that the god Liber is my father.'4 We applauded Trimalchio's phrase, and kissed the boy heartily as he went round.

"After this dish Trimalchio got up and retired. With the tyrant away we had our freedom, and we began to draw the conversation with our neighbours. Damas began after calling for bumpers: 'Day is nothing, Night is on you before you can turn round. Then there is no better plan than going straight out of bed to dinner. It is precious cold. I could scarcely get warm in a bath. But a hot drink is as good as an overcoat. I have taken some strong drink and I'm just too mellow. The wine's gone to my head.'"

At this point, their host being absent, there follows a mass of gossip about local characters and acquaintances, most of them newly-rich and thoroughly disreputable. But since there is little or nothing relevant to wine we may pass on. Chatter it was, and chatter, "until Trimalchio came in mopping his brow, and washed his hands in scent. After a short pause, he said, 'You will excuse me, gentlemen? My bowels have not been working for several days. All the doctors are puzzled. Still, I found pomegranate rind useful, and pinewood boiled in vinegar. I hope now my stomach will learn to observe its old decencies. Besides, I have such rumblings inside me you would think there was a bull there. So if any of you gentlemen wishes to retire there is no need to be shy about it. We were none of us born quite solid. I cannot imagine any torture like holding oneself in. The one thing Jupiter himself cannot forbid is that we should have relief. Why do you laugh, Fortunata; it is you who are always keeping me awake all night. Of course, as far as I am concerned, anyone may relieve himself in the dining room. The doctors forbid retention. But if the matter is serious, everything is ready outside; water, towels,

4 The name of the god Liber was quite wrongly derived from the fact that wine frees men from cares. Trimalchio, who frees slaves, therefore takes him as his patron or father; and see p. 156 above.

and all the other little comforts. Take my word for it, vapours go
to the brain and make a disturbance throughout the body. I know
many people have died this way, by refusing to admit the truth
to themselves.' We thanked him for his generosity and kindness,
and then tried to suppress our laughter by drinking hard and fast.
We did not yet realise that we had only got halfway through the
delicacies, and still had an uphill task before us, as they say. The
tables were cleared to the sound of music. Trimalchio turned to
us with a mild expression and said, 'I will change the wine if you
do not like it. You will have to give it its virtues. By the goodness
of the gods I do not have to buy it. Anything here which makes
your mouths water is grown on a country estate of mine which I
know nothing about as yet. I believe it is on the boundary of
Terracina and Tarentum. Just now I want to join up all Sicily
with properties of mine, so that if I take a fancy to go to Africa
I shall travel through my own land. But do tell me, Agamemnon,
what declamation did you deliver in school today? Of course, I
do not practise in court myself, but I learned literature for
domestic purposes. And do not imagine that I despise learning.
I have got two libraries, one Greek and one Latin. Tell me, dear
Agamemnon,' said Trimalchio, 'do you know anything of the
twelve labours of Hercules, or the story of Ulysses and how the
Cyclops twisted his thumb with the tongs? I used to read these
things in Homer when I was a boy. Yes, and I myself with my
own eyes saw the Sibyl of Cumae hanging in a cage; and when
the Greek boys cried at her: "Sibyl, Sibyl, what do you want?"
she used to answer, "I would that I were dead." I am the sole
owner,' he continued, 'of genuine Corinthian plate.' I thought he
would boast with his usual cheek that he had cups imported
direct from Corinth. But he went one better: 'You may perhaps
inquire,' said he, 'how I come to be alone in having genuine
Corinthian stuff; the obvious reason is that the name of the dealer
I buy it from is Corinthus. But what is real Corinthian, unless a
man has Corinthus at his back? Do not imagine that I am an
ignoramus. I know perfectly well how Corinthian plate was first
brought into the world. At the fall of Ilium, Hannibal, a trickster

and a great knave, collected all the sculptures, bronze, gold, and silver, into a single pile, and set light to them. They all melted into one amalgam of bronze. The workmen took bits out of this lump and made plates and entrée dishes and statuettes. That is how Corinthian metal was born, from all sorts lumped together, neither one kind nor the other. You will forgive me if I say that personally I prefer glass; glass at least does not smell. If it were not so fragile I'd prefer it to gold; but it's cheap. There was once a workman who made an unbreakable glass cup. He got an audience with the Emperor with his invention, asked Caesar to give it back to him and then threw it on the floor. Caesar was as frightened as could be. But the man picked up his cup from the ground: it was dinted like a bronze bowl; then he took a little hammer out of his pouch and made the cup quite sound again without any trouble. After this he thought he had himself seated on the throne of Jupiter, especially when Caesar asked him: "does anyone else know how to blow glass like this?" Just see what happened. He said, "no!" and then Caesar had him beheaded. Why? Because if his invention were generally known we should treat gold like dirt. Myself I have a great passion for silver. I own about a hundred four-gallon cups engraved with Cassandra killing her children, and they lying there dead in the most life-like way. I have a thousand jugs which Mummius left to my patron, and on them you see Daedalus shutting Niobe into the Trojan horse. And I have got the fights between Hermeros and Petraites on my cups, and every cup is a heavy one; for I won't part with my treasures, not for any money.'

"Then Trimalchio shouted, 'Out with water! In with wine!' We took up the joke, especially Agamemnon, who knew how to earn a second invitation to dinner. Trimalchio warmed to his drinking under our flattery, and was almost drunk when he said: 'None of you ask my dear Fortunata to dance. Listen, no one can dance the cancan better.' He then lifted his hands above his head and gave us a caricature of the actor Syrus, while all the servants sang in chorus. But a clerk ruined his passion for the dance by reading, as though from the gazette: 'July the 26th. Thirty boys and forty girls were born on Trimalchio's estate at Cumae. Five hundred oxen were broken in to the plough. On the same date: the slave Mithridates was led to crucifixion for having damned the soul of our lord Gaius Trimalchio. On the same date: ten million sesterces which could not be invested were returned to the reserve. On the same day: there was a fire in our gardens at Pompeii, which broke out in the house of Nasta the bailiff.' 'Stop', said Trimalchio. 'When did I buy any gardens at Pompeii?' 'Last year,' said the clerk, 'so that they are not entered in your accounts yet.'"

Suddenly there started something like an acrobatic "floor-show" but the reader can hardly fail to observe its inferiority to the Athenian fifth-century "floor-show" described in our first chapter.

"A dull fool stood there with a ladder and made a boy dance from rung to rung and on to the very top to the music of popular airs, and then made him hop through burning hoops, and pick up a wine jar with his teeth. No one was impressed by this except Trimalchio, who kept saying that it was a thankless occupation. There were only two things in the world that he could watch with real pleasure, acrobats and trumpeters; all the other shows were silly nonsense. 'Why,' said he, 'I once bought a whole comedy company, but I preferred them to do Atellane plays and I told my flute-player to have Latin songs. What men do not look for turns about and comes to pass. And high above us Fortune directs our affairs. Wherefore, slave, hand us Falernian wine.'

"It was only natural that among such a company where all had drunk too much a phase of quarrelsomeness should begin to appear; but the host interrupted it neatly with the words: 'Come let us do better and start the fun over again, and have a look at these Homer fellows.' A troop came in at once and clashed spear on shield. Trimalchio himself sat up on his cushion, and when the actors talked to each other in Greek verse, as their conceited way is, he intoned Latin from a book. Soon there was silence, and he said, 'You know the story they are doing? Diomede and Ganymede were two brothers. Their sister was Helen. Agamemnon carried her off and took in Diana by sacrificing a deer to her instead. And so now Homer is telling the tale of war between Troy and Parentium. Of course he won and married his daughter Iphigenia to Achilles. That drove Ajax mad, and he will show you the story in a minute.' As he spoke the heroes raised a shout, and the slaves stood back to let a boiled calf on a presentation dish be brought in. There was a helmet on its head. Ajax followed and attacked it with his sword drawn as if he were mad; and after making passes with the edge and the flat he collected slices on the point, and divided the calf among the astonished company.

"We were not given long to admire these elegant *tours de force*; suddenly there came a noise from the ceiling, and the whole dining-room trembled. I rose from my place in a panic: I was afraid some acrobat would come down through the roof. All the other guests too looked up astonished, wondering what the new portent from heaven announced. The whole ceiling parted asunder, and an enormous hoop, apparently knocked out of a giant cask, was let down. All round it were hung golden crowns and alabaster boxes of perfumes. We were told to take these away as presents for ourselves. Then I looked back at the central table. A dish with some cakes on it had now appeared with a Priapus made by the pastry-cook standing in the middle, holding up every kind of fruit and grapes in his wide apron in the conventional style. Greedily we reached for his treasures, and a sudden fresh turn of humour renewed our merriment. All the cakes and all the fruits, however lightly they were touched, began to spurt out saffron, and the nasty juice flew even into our mouths. We thought it must be a sacred dish that was anointed with such holy appointments, and we all stood straight up and cried, 'The Gods bless Augustus, Father of his country.' But as some people even after this solemnity snatched at the fruit, we filled our napkins too, myself especially, for I thought that I could never fill Giton's lap with enough presents. And now three boys with their white tunics well tucked up came in and two of them put images of the Lares with lockets round their necks on the table, while one carried round a bowl of wine and cried, 'May the Gods be propitious!'

"Trimalchio said that one of the images was called Gain, another Luck, and the third Profit. And as everybody else kissed Trimalchio's true portrait we were ashamed to pass it by."

And now several of the guests began to tell ghost stories, which cast an atmosphere of gloom over the party, when suddenly a policeman knocked at the dining-room door, "and a man dressed in white for some festivity came in with a number of others. I was frightened by his solemn looks, and thought the chief constable had arrived. So I tried to get up and plant my bare feet on the ground. Agamemnon laughed at my anxiety and said, 'Control yourself, you silly fool! It is Habinnas of the priests' college, a monumental mason with a reputation for making first-class tombstones.' Relieved by this news, I lay down in my place again, and watched Habinnas' entrance with great astonishment. He was quite drunk, and had put his hands on his wife's shoulders; he had several wreaths on, and ointment was running down his forehead into his eyes. He sat down in the chief magistrate's place, and at once asked for wine and hot water. Trimalchio was delighted at his good humour, and demanded a larger cup for himself, and asked him how he had been received. 'We had everything there except you,' was the reply, 'for my eyes were here with you. Yes, it was really splendid. Scissa was having a funeral feast on the ninth day for her poor dear slave, whom she set free on his death-bed. And I believe she will have an enormous sum to pay the tax-collector, for they reckon that the dead man was worth fifty thousand. But anyhow it was a pleasant affair, even if we did have to pour half our drinks over his lamented bones.' 'Ah,' said Trimalchio, 'but what did you have for dinner?' 'I will tell you if I can,' he said, 'but my memory is in such a fine way that I often forget my own name. Well, first we had a pig crowned with a wine-cup, garnished with honey cakes, and liver very well done, and beetroot of course, and pure wholemeal bread, which I prefer to white myself; it puts strength into you, and is good for the bowels. The next dish was cold tart, with excellent Spanish wine poured over warm honey. Indeed I ate a lot of the tart, and gave myself such a soaking of honey. Peas and lupines were handed, choice of nuts and an apple each. I took two myself, and I have got them here tied up in my napkin: for if I do not bring some present back for my pet slave-boy I'll get into trouble. Oh, good, my wife reminds me. There was a piece of bear on a side dish. Scintilla was rash enough to taste it, and nearly vomited up her own guts. I ate over a pound myself, for it tasted just like wild boar. What I say is, as bears eat up us poor men, how much better right has a poor man to eat up a bear? Finally we had cheese mellowed in new wine. But tell me, Gaius, why is Fortunata not at dinner?' At a given signal, all the slaves called Fortunata four times and more. So she came in with a high yellow waist-band on, fitted so as to let a cherry-red bodice appear under it, and twisted anklets, and gold-embroidered white shoes. She wiped her hands on a scarf which she had round her neck, plumped down on the couch, where Scintilla, Habinnas's wife, was lying, kissed her as she was clapping her hands, and said, 'Is it really you that I see?'

"Meanwhile the tipsy wives laughed together, and gave each other drunken kisses, one prating of her prudence as a housewife, the other of the favourites of her husband and his inattention to her. While they were hugging each other, Habinnas got up quickly, took Fortunata by the legs, and threw her over on the sofa. 'Oh, oh,' she shouted as her dress flew up over her knees. She took refuge in Scintilla's bosom, and buried her burning face in a napkin.

"After a while, Trimalchio ordered fresh helpings of food to be served. The servants took away all the tables, brought others, and sprinkled about sawdust coloured with saffron and vermilion, and, what I had never seen before, powdered mica. Promptly Trimalchio said, 'I might really be satisfied with this course, as you've got your fresh helpings. But if there is anything nice, put it on.'"

The gluttonous, bibulous, comical story flows on; the host reads out his will, appoints the arrangements of his burial and tomb-stone. He weeps, Fortunata weeps, Habinnas weeps, all the slaves weep. More drink, more quarrels, ugly little episodes, but wildly funny as told by Petronius. Trimalchio, hopelessly drunk, and thinking he is dying, calls for trumpeters to blow a solemn "dead march" over his prostrate form. Dawn is breaking, the trumpets seem to some passer-by a fire-alarm, and the Brigade is called. They break in the doors with their axes and drench all and sundry with water. In all this confusion Encolpius, his brother Ascyltos and the catamite Giton slip away from the mad-house of the multi-millionaire, Trimalchio.

Thus and thus things could happen in Italy in the baneful days of a Gaius, a Claudius, or a Nero; yet it is certain that after the vulgarities and debaucheries that characterised the Neronian reign, life in the Empire, in Italy, in Rome itself reverted to some-thing more steady and simple under bourgeois emperors like Vespasian and Titus, under provincial soldiers like Trajan and Hadrian and Antoninus. By the time that Rome was ruled by an imperial philosopher like Marcus Aurelius it was evident that such absurdities and vulgarities as the Banquet of Trimalchio had vanished from the ways of life. Nevertheless few will be found to deny that there is far more entertainment to be derived from the *Satyricon* of Gaius Petronius Arbiter than from the *Meditations* of Marcus Aurelius Antoninus.

When the Emperor Constantine switched over from official paganism to official Christianity there was, at first, no special change of emphasis, as the coinage alone can prove.[5] It took a long time before the pagan Victoria took over the personification of an archangel. Socially, of course, the powerful and celibate patriarchs and bishops of Christendom—soon to be supported by mad, fanatical monks—launched their attacks against Aphro-dite. Love, loveliness, beauty, nakedness, the glories of sexual passion and of art were all "works of the Devil". They signi-fied depravity, perdition, horror; for had not many Fathers of the Church concurred in the view that woman was utterly

5 And see especially M. P. Nilsson, "Pagan Divine Service in Late Antiquity", *Harvard Theological Review*, Vol. 38 (1945).

abominable? From this belief the misogynist misery of mediaeval Europe was bred.

At first it may seem a matter of no little surprise that the new dispensation which so feared and hated Aphrodite and her son Eros, did not ban what Dionysos represented. Quite late in the history of Christendom an anti-Dionysiac profession was evolved; not, however, by Catholics but by oddly fanatical Protestants, some of whom survive to this day.

An historian confronted by two opposing views may wonder which way of life is to be preferred: the once-serious Moslem practice involving a plenitude of women, but no wine; or the serious monastic Catholic practice permitting plenty of wine but no women. The ancient Greeks had the answer, later to be forgotten. "Nothing in excess." A fair amount of love, a fair amount of wine. But never too much.

✤✤✤✤✤✤✤✤✤✤✤✤✤✤✤✤✤✤✤✤✤✤✤✤✤✤✤✤✤✤✤✤✤✤✤✤✤✤✤

## Chapter Twelve

# CONTINUITY

✤✤✤✤✤✤✤✤✤✤✤✤✤✤✤✤✤✤✤✤✤✤✤✤✤✤✤✤✤✤✤✤✤✤✤✤✤✤✤

HOW much of the ancient world—and especially of the ancient
Greek world—still survives? There are, of course, the unsurpassed monuments—temples, statues, lovely vases, perfect coins,
and all the other dainty works of art that can be seen and touched.
There is the splendour of an ancient literature from Homer
onward that can still inspire and intoxicate a part, at least, of mankind. But what of the personal, vivid and religious emotion of
ancient Greece? How much has prevailed against the pietist,
restrictive impositions of fifth- and sixth-century Christendom?
The answer is that a very great deal has prevailed. Dionysos, fat
Seilenos, Pan, goat-legged Satyrs, Nymphs are still around and
about in Greece. More than that, even Aphrodite and her son
Eros—of all deities most feared by a great community once
soaked in sex-hatred—persist. A well-known modern tale about
them may serve as an introduction to our story before we move
to consider the Beings more intimately connected with wine.

Once upon a time there was a very beautiful queen, by name
Aphrodite, who had a castle at Daphni (half-way on the road from
Athens to Eleusis) and also owned the heights of Acro-Corinth; these
two places she had caused to be connected by a subterranean way
which passed under the sea. Now there were two kings both of whom
were smitten with her beauty and sought her hand in marriage. She
herself favoured one of them and hated the other; but not wishing to

declare her preference and so arouse the anger of the rejected suitor, she announced that she was about to build a palace on the height of Acro-Corinth, and would set her suitors each a task to perform; one should build the fortifications round the summit, the other should sink a well to provide the castle with water; and she promised her hand to the suitor who should first complete his task. Now she supposed the sinking of the well to be the lighter task and therefore assigned it to the suitor whom she favoured; but he met with unforeseen difficulties, and his rival meanwhile made steady progress with the walls. At last they were wellnigh built, and it remained only to put in place the keystone over the main gate. Then Aphrodite, marking the danger, went with winning words and smiles and bade the builder lay aside his tools, for the prize was now safely in his grasp, and led him away to a grassy spot where she beguiled him so long with tender words and caresses, that the other suitor meanwhile redoubling his efforts pierced the rock and found water in plenty.

Not far from Daphni one may still see the foundations of a temple of Aphrodite; and it is well known that all the summit of Acrocorinth was hers in those remote days when her girl-votaries lived there.[1]

In this tale the goddess herself makes love to mortal men; and in such high thoughts the early Fathers of the Church—foremost among them the renegade Clement of Alexandria—found only evil.

This champion of Christianity knew no chivalry, gave no quarter, disdained no weapon, held no method of attack too base or insidious, if only he could wound and crush his heathen foes. It was his part to pervert, to degrade, to blaspheme their whole religion; and that which they held most sacred was marked out for his most virulent scorn. Naturally to those who drew near with pure and reverent minds the mysteries wore a very different aspect. That which Clement misnamed lust, they felt to be love; where he saw only degradation, they recognised a wonderful condescension of their gods.[2]

[1] See J. C. Lawson, *Modern Greek Folklore and Ancient Greek Religion* (1910), pp. 117 f.
[2] Lawson, *op. cit.*, p. 572.

Clement, in his own day, led an organised campaign of calumny against all that was held most sacred in the ancient pagan world. Yet after a while the Eastern Church sought, much more than did the Western, to adapt itself to the invincible belief of its age-old precursors, and conciliation can only lead to compromise.

It was politic no doubt to encourage the weaker brethren by building churches on sites where they had long been wont to worship: it was politic to smooth the path of the common folk by substituting for the god whom they had worshipped a patron-saint of like name or attributes. But in so doing the Church practically condoned polytheism. She drove out the old gods from their temples made with hands, but did not ensure the obliteration of them from men's hearts. The saints whom she set up in the place of the old deities were certain to acquire the rank of gods in the estimation of the people and, despite the niceties of ecclesiastical doctrine, to become in fact objects of frank and open worship. The adoption of the old places of worship made it inevitable that the old associations of the pagan cults should survive and blend themselves with the new ideas, and that the churches should more often acquire prestige from their heathen sites than themselves shed a new lustre of sanctity upon them. In effect, paganism was not uprooted to make room for the planting of Christianity, but served rather as ar old stock on which a new and vigorous branch, . . . owing its very vitality to alien sap, might be engrafted. Bitterly and despondently did the early Fathers of the Church, and above all John Chrysostom, complain of the inveteracy of pagan customs within the pale of the Church, while a kind of official recognition was given to many superstitions which were clearly outside the pale.[3]

Fisher-folk, islanders, peasants in Greece of today may profess and call themselves Christians; but under the surface they are as pagan and as polytheistic in their hearts as were their ancestors because by their acceptance of Christendom with its saints they have not diminished the number of their gods. All this comes through in the tales we still know about the God of Wine and his votaries.

[3] Lawson, *op. cit.*, p. 41.

In the island of Naxos[4] once devoted to the worship of Dionysos, popular tradition ascribes to Saint Dionysius the introduction of the grape; while in the neighbouring isle of Paros, Saint George is worshipped under the title of the "drunkard" (*Methystes*), because his festival there on the 15th November is the signal for broaching the new wine. The story of the introduction of the grape to Naxos is told as follows:

When Dionysius was still young, he made a journey through Greece in order to cross to Naxos. Being tired upon his way, he sat down upon a stone to rest. As he sat there, he perceived a very small plant growing in the ground before him, which appeared to him so beautiful that he determined to take it with him, to plant there. But fearing lest the heat of the sun should wither it before he got to Naxos, he placed it in the thigh-bone of a bird, the better to carry it. As he went on, however, the plant grew so rapidly in the hand of the saint that the shoots came out at either end of the bone. Fearing anew that it would wither in the sun, he cast about what he should do, and finding the thigh-bone of a lion he inserted into this the plant with the other bone. But it still grew and filled the lion's bone. Then he lit on the skull of an ass, and into this he slipped the two other bones with the plant, and so brought it safely to Naxos. But when he came to plant it the roots were so firmly fixed in the bones that he was forced to plant bones and root together. The plant grew and prospered and bore magnificent grapes, and from these they made the first wine, and the saint gave it men to drink. And then the wonder of it was that when they had drunk a little they sang like birds, when they drank more they grew strong as lions, but then if they drank yet more they became like asses.[5]

One is once more reminded of Silenus and the Bacchic rout of jollity in the curious mediaeval cult at Naxos of Saint Pachys

---

4 The story is taken from a book by Rennell Rodd, *The Customs and Lore of Modern Greece*, p. 142 (Stott, London, 1892). Note that the same story is recounted by Lawson, *op. cit.*, p. 43.

5 The ass is especially the sacred animal of Dionysos who appears seated upon its back on the coinage of Mende; see above p. 68.

(Saint Fat), a saint whose intervention was held to confer the desirable gift of obesity, a quality which must have been much esteemed in the early Middle Ages, seeing what work the Duke Marco Sanudo had to put this worship down. He, having taken possession in 1207 of the island, founded the Duchy of the Aegean Sea, built a splendid castle, and, as a good Catholic, set about the abolition of a cult that savoured of antique paganism.

Difficulties such as never existed in the ancient world concerning nakedness have become endemic in the Eastern Church which has forced prudery on the people's bodies though not on their minds. Maenads or Thyiads, ready to appear unclothed, or nearly so, would not be found in Greece today. And yet there does exist in what was once ancient Thrace, perhaps the original home of Bacchos himself, a practice which has kinship with ancient ways. Dionysos was god of all fertile and life-giving fluids including rain, for he was in a fashion, as son of Zeus Almighty, his deputy on earth. That is why even today a girl wearing corn and vine-leaves may appear once in a while as a ministrant of the fertility god. Among the Vlachs of that region, who are apt to be classed as gypsies because of their nomadic habits, but who are denizens of the Thraco-Macedonian area, it is the custom to choose a girl as "rain-maker". She is stripped and goes naked except for a short skirt of corn and vines. Girls thus scantily attired go from house to house and are drenched by people with buckets of water. The ceremony used to occur regularly on the third Tuesday after Easter, but may be repeated during summer at any time of drought.[6] There is something about this strange custom existing in the heart of what once was Thrace that cannot fail to recall the wilder maenads of the ancient world. Mountain and meadow, sea-shore and the rolling flowery hills of Arcadia, island uplands and sands glittering in moonlight, all these—so the peasants and fisher-folk will tell you—are still inhabited by supernatural beings; nymphs, satyrs and Pan. They have seen them and some of us have seen them too. Nymphs are no longer known by that name since in modern Greek

[6] J. G. Frazer, *Golden Bough, The Magic Art*, i, 273 f.

*Nymphé* means a bride, and so these lovely feminine spirits of the Wild are all called Nereids today. If they are conceived as belonging to certain caves, or trees, springs, streams or the sea they still are Nereids.

The late John Cuthbert Lawson, Fellow of Pembroke College, Honorary Commander in the Greek Navy during the First World War, whose lectures I, as an undergraduate, had the good fortune to attend, was a calm and very level-headed man. He wrote as follows:

I myself once had a Nereid pointed out to me by my guide, and there certainly was the semblance of a female figure draped in white and tall beyond human stature flitting in the dusk between the gnarled and twisted boles of an old olive-yard. What the apparition was, I had no leisure to investigate; for my guide with many signs of the cross and muttered invocations of the Virgin urged my mule to perilous haste along the rough mountain-path. But had I inherited, as he, a belief in Nereids together with a fertile gift of mendacity, I should doubtless have corroborated the highly-coloured story which he told when we reached the light and safety of the next village; and the ready acceptance of the story by those who heard it proved to me that a personal encounter with Nereids was really reckoned among the possible incidents of every-day life.

Indeed I am very ready to believe him, partly because he once told me that he had seen a Nereid, partly because of what I myself have seen, in Greece. But we must follow more of Lawson's account of Nereids in modern lore.

The Nereids are conceived as women half-divine yet not immortal, always young, always beautiful, capricious at best, and at their worst cruel. Of all that is light and mirthful they are the ideal; of all that is lovely the exquisite embodiment; and their hearts beneath are ever swayed by fierce gusts of love and of hate.

The beauty of the Nereids, the sweetness of their voices, and the grace and litheness of their movements have given rise to many familiar phrases which are eloquent of feelings other than awe in the people's minds. "She is fair as a Nereid", "she has the eyes, the arms, the bosom of a Nereid", "she sings, she dances, like a Nereid"—such are the compliments time and again passed upon a bride, whose white dress and ornaments of gold seem to complete the resemblance. Possibly the twofold usage in antiquity of the word *Nymphé* is responsible for a still surviving association of bridal dress with the Nereids; it is at any rate to the peasants' minds an incontestable fact that white and gold are the colours chiefly affected by Nereids in their dress.[7]

Human votaries were not the sole participants in the rout of Dionysos, for Maenads and bacchoi and bacchai were joined betimes by such half-divine creatures as nymphs and satyrs and Pan. It is many years now since I saw him, but I make bold to state that I once saw a satyr on Mount Parnassus. In the year 1925 we were a party of four at Delphi where we spent some days, and in late April a visit to the Corycian Cave is a most memorable event. My wife and I had been there two years before and I could have found my way to it with ease. But the rather nervous Cambridge don and the rather vague school-master between them advocated obtaining the services of the Parnassus guide, George Mourtsos, today an old man tough as a walnut, one of my best friends in Greece, who can still climb the mountain and put youngsters to shame.[8] We set out in perfect weather up the "Bad Stair",[9] and reached the splendid rolling plain 4000 feet above sea level (Pl. XVI). After a drink at one of those enchanting ice-cold springs of water, and after a rest, we began to move in an easterly direction. Don and "Mr Chips" would talk when they should have used eyes, not tongues; my wife was a friendly listener to their learned chatter. George Mourtsos, who had crossed himself three times, as we started out for the cave, hung back. Before long I found myself walking far ahead of the other four; half a mile in advance of them; silent, no distinct thoughts, but the mystic, the numinous was taking possession of my being.

And then suddenly I saw HIM. Anemones and cyclamen, and smaller flowers were shining in hollows that held dark-brown

7 Lawson, *op. cit.*, pp. 131 ff.
8 I last met him at Delphi in April 1956.
9 See p. 107 above.

soil and glitter-white stones; other hollows held in their depths
the last cushions of winter snow, still unmelted. Trees were sparse
where my route lay, but there were cedars and mountain pines
and a few small hesitant beeches veiled in pale-green. Against this
setting the satyr was very clear and quite solid. Matted black hair,
long pointed ears, a sturdy muscular body deep red-brown of tan,
hairy, and still more hairy where the thighs began to be merged
into goat-legs ending in hooves. A black tail; I took it all in as he
trotted across my path not twenty yards away. I stopped and he
stopped, and both looked at one another. Never have I seen such
fear in eyes except, perhaps, in the eyes of a trembling spaniel.
Suddenly he drummed on his chest with clenched fists, turned and
ran straight for the trunk of a large cedar. Filled now with delight
and curiosity I walked silently and as quickly as I dared up to that
tree and round it. No satyr to be seen. That was a reality. About
Pan I am not so sure but the tale may be worth telling.

The year was 1930, the time late April, the place in the north-
east corner of Peloponnesus, where the lands of Argos and
Corinth march. Five of us were being driven north towards
Corinth on a stretch of road which twenty-six years ago was
pock-marked with huge pot-holes. Today that same roadway is
excellent, but then five miles an hour was the only sensible speed
for the springs of a car and the jarred spines of passengers. On our
right there rose a steep sandstone bank some twelve feet above the
road surface; and on top of the bank was a rich lay-out of small,
well-trenched vines, while along the very edge of the bank there
grew a little hedge of green barley. Behind this hedge and among
the vines HE showed himself. He was a Hellenistic, little-boy Pan.
Had he been human one would have said a little seven-year-old.
Black rough hair, very pointed ears, a snub nose and a body
beautifully shaped, and coloured by the sun to a deep chocolate
cream. He was naked to the waist. Perhaps he was really human
and wore shorts, but the young barley and the vines concealed
the lower half of him as he skipped along the ridge beside our
slow-moving car. In one hand he held a small curved piece of
stick; in the other a little syrinx, or "Pan pipes", on which he

blew a tinny tune. Had he the legs of a little goat? We never knew. But he cried out to us in the car in a voice high-pitched but of astonishing strength: "Chorēzete, chorēzete; sas kamnō mousika!" A strange mixture of ancient and modern Greek? Or just a local dialect? But the meaning was clear enough: "Dance all of you, dance; I am making music for you."

Two of us in the party—my wife and myself—saw and heard all this quite distinctly. The others, being torpid and tired, seem not to have registered any impression of the episode. At this point it is not easy to express one's reactions and emotions. What should like to say, in view of my own limited personal experiences, is that one need not treat as pure fancy or pure imagination impressions that some living travellers and very many Greeks themselves have received of the presence of strange creatures of the ancient world still perceptible in the world of today. We can perhaps say with a great poet[10]: "Fear came upon me . . . then a spirit passed before my face; the hair of my flesh stood up. It stood still but I could not discern the form thereof: an image was before mine eyes; there was silence and I heard a voice saying, Shall mortal man be more just than God?"

It has been a pleasing diversion to write this little book, even in the knowledge that much has been left unsaid and that many a gap is left unfilled. The topic is one which could have been made burdensome with piled statistics and given the savour of heavy sweet wine or the aridity of wine turned to vinegar. Better to let gaiety reign around this gladdening subject. And so we have observed civilised and vulgar banqueteers, one lot in Athenian, the other lot in Roman settings; have sought the first home of the grape, and its uses among Homer's heroes prefiguring the usages of Greeks, Romans and their many successors down to this day. Digressions have exerted their inevitable pull, calling for notes on the variety of containers for ancient wine, the many songs sung at wine parties, and the bibulous ways of women in

[10] *Job* iv, 14 ff.

Athens. Not least among entertaining events in history was the fearful impact of the cult of the Wine-god in the second century B.C. upon the correct and puritanical Romans. Bacchos—Bacchus to the Romans—delivered a fantastic shock.

Twelve Gods; and then a thirteenth—Dionysos Bromios Bacchos—to join the others in that splendid godly gang, superb in its total lack of inhibitions. The profound difference between Gods and men lies in the fact that Gods dare break man-made rules, whereas men dare not. And when a man goes mad and thinks he is God, and throws away the maxims of the golden rule, total disaster awaits him as the Greek tragedians knew. "Never exceed", "the mean is best" "know yourself". Those are rules for mortals; but Gods may and do ignore them. That, in a sense, is the dominant theme of Euripides' *Bacchae*. Better not fight against Bromios. God is very dangerous. No greater human folly prevails than an assumption that God has subjected Himself to rules, laws, dictates devised for the regulation of His creatures. Above all He must never be defined. It is the attempt to define Him that turns almost all dogma into a kind of blasphemy. The Wine-god can and does release mankind from presumptuous *credos* about God, His Father. Once upon a time—we thought— He may have been born a peasant-god of wine and corn, millennia ago in Anatolia; but when He reached Greece a Corn-goddess, Demeter, was already present. So Dionysos Bacchos was gradually conceived of as God of all life-giving fluids and as centred on a "creation", a "creature", a "creature-comfort", the GRAPE.

# A SHORT BIBLIOGRAPHY

I    Among ancient writers, Athenaeus, Cato, Varro, Columella and Pliny are the most important. Strabo also provides information, as does Livy on the Bacchanals.

## DICTIONARIES

II    (*a*) W. Smith, W. Wayte and G. E. Marindin, *A Dictionary of Greek and Roman Antiquities*, Vol. ii (1891), Article *Vinum*.

(*b*) Daremberg et Saglio, *Dictionnaire des Antiquitése*, Vol. ix (1912), article *Vinum*, pp. 912 ff. (Note: the monumental German *Reallexicon der Altertumswissenschaft* has not yet got to the topic of "Wein".)

## MODERN WORKS

III    Couanon, Georges. "Les Vins et Eaux-de-vie de vin de France", 1. *La Vigne à travers les âges* (Paris, 1920).

Henderson, A. *The History of Ancient and Modern Wine* (London, 1824).

Labaste, A. "Les Vins grecs", *Annales de Géographie*, Tome XLIX (Paris, 1939).

Lutz, H. F. *Viticulture and Brewing in the Ancient Orient* (Leipzig, 1922).

Molyneux, E. "Grape Growing for Amateurs", *Baʒaar, Exchange and Mart* (London, 1922).

Perrin, Armand. *La Civilisation de la vigne*: Pt. I, Origine et aspect actuel des vignobles; Pt. II, Les Techniques de la vigne; Pt. III, Les Conditions Sociales (1938).

Remark, P. *Der Weinbau im Römerreich* (Munchen, 1927).

Ricci, C. *La Coltura della vite e la fabbricaʒione del vino nell' Egitto greco-romano* (Milan, 1924).

Reichter, W. *Der Weinbau im römischen Altertum* (Schaffhausen, 1932).

Zapletal, V. "Der Wein in der Bibel", *Biblische Studien*, Heft 1 (Freiburg i. B. 1920).

IV The following are admirable for a study of the shapes of and paintings on ancient Greek vases.

(*a*) E. Pfuhl and J. D. Beazley, *Masterpieces of Greek Drawing and Painting* (New Edition, 1955).

(*b*) G. M. A. Richter and M. J. Milne, *Shapes and Names of Athenian Vases* (New York, 1935).

(*c*) The great series of fascicules of the *Corpus Vasorum Antiquorum* illustrating vases in a great number of collections.

V The following abbreviations are used:
*A.G.A.* = Charles Seltman, *Approach to Greek Art*, 1948.
*B.S.A.* = *Annual of the British School at Athens.*
*F.R.* = A. Furtwängler and K. Reichhold, *Griechische Vasenmalerei* (Munich, 1904) (continued by F. Hauser and E. Buschor).
*J.H.S.* = *Journal of Hellenic Studies.*

# Index

Achaea, Achaeans, 37–8, 42–3
Achilles, 32–3, 35–40, 43, 50, 116, 118
shield of, 33
Acrocorinth, 67, 173–4
Acropolis, 67, 103–4, 109, 114
Adonis, 26
Adriatic, 74
Aebutius, Publius, 145–6
Aegean, 130, 133, 138, 141
Duchy of, 177
Aeolis, 133
Aeschylus, 54
Africa, 156, 165
North, 136
Agamemnon, 32, 35, 37, 42, 44, 96, 168
Agamemnon (teacher), 159, 165–6, 169
Agathias Scholasticus, 126–7
Agathon, 98
Agave, 55, 58–61
Agay, 136
Ajax, 168
Akragas, 92
Albanum, Alban, Mons Albanus, 153–4
Albenga, 136
Alcaeus, 127
Alcinous, 41
Alcmaeonidae, Alcmaeonids, 105, 114–15
Alcohol, 71
Alexander, 25, 27–8, 96, 115, 118
Alexandria, Alexandrians, 117, 134–135, 157, 161
Algeria, 156
Alkman, 117
Alpheus, 137
Alsace, 157
Amasis painter, 69–70

America, American, 129, 160
Ammon, Ammonites, 19
Amphissa, 108
Amphora, 69, 152
Amphoreus Metrétés, 136–7
Amyclae, 153
*Anabasis* (Xenophon), 20
Anacreon, 117, 127
Anatolia, Anatolian, 21, 24–5, 27–8, 30–1, 50, 52, 141, 152, 156, 182
*see also* Asia Minor
Andritsaena, 137–8
Angela of Foligno (Bl.), 63–4
Antenor, 115
Antheon, 136
Antibes, 130
Antikythera, 129
Antimachus, 120–1
Antinous (Homeric), 42
Antinous (lover of Hadrian), 123
Antipater, 121
Antipolis (Antibes), 143
Antisthenes, 6
Antoninus, 171
Antony, Mark, 123
Apelles, 45
Aphrodite, 8, 22, 26, 57, 120, 124–126, 131, 171–4
*see also* Cypris: Pandemos
Apollo, 35, 46, 50, 100, 102, 106
Arabic, Arabian, 16, 151
Arachova, 105
Aramaic, 25
Ararat, 16–17
Arbiter of Taste, 159
Arcadia, 113, 137–8, 177
Archeades, 120
Archelaus, 54, 61
Ares, 50
Arete, 41
Argos, 37, 180

Ariadne, 9, 10, 13, 34, 49, 94
Ariousia, 77
Aristodemus, 91
Aristogeiton, 114–16
Aristophanes, 97
   *see also* Lysistrata: Thesmophori-
   azusae
Aristotle, 39
Ark, Noah's, 16
Armagnac, 143
Armenia, Armenian, 15, 20
Arsinous, 43
Artemis, 99
Artemision, 136
Asclepiades (of Myrlea), 45
Ascyltos, 159, 171
Asia, 15, 55, 62
Asia Minor, 15, 23–5, 27, 35, 55, 141
   *see also* Anatolia
Asklepiades (of Samos), 118–20
Asklepios, 43, 157
Atellane plays, 167
Athenaeus, 117, 131–2, 138, 141, 157
Athena, Athene, 22, 41, 50, 103, 109,
   112–13, 116, 125, 131–2
Athens, Athenian, Attic, 1, 2, 10–14,
   27, 31, 54, 61–2, 67, 79, 82–3,
   87, 91–2, 94–7, 101–9, 112–16,
   132, 135–7, 157, 173, 181–2
   *see also* Attica
Atlantic, 129
Attica, 62, 129, 133
Augustus, Augustan, 122, 144, 153,
   156, 168
Autolykos, 2, 3, 9, 10
Autonoe, 58
Ayesha, 151
Aztecs, 40

Ba'al-tars, 25
Babylon, 125
Babylonian captivity, 16
*Bacchae* (Euripides), 54–5, 102, 107–
   108, 149, 182
Bacchanalians, Bacchanals, 145–8,
   152

Bacchant(e)s, 26, 59, 60, 64–5, 149
Bacchos, Bacchus, Bacchic, 9, 26,
   40, 49–66, 101–2, 107, 117,
   122–3, 144, 148–9, 151, 156–
   157, 163, 176–7, 182
   *see also* Bromios: Dionysos
Bacchai, Bacchoi, 49–66 passim,
   106, 179
Bactria, 21
Bad Stair, 107, 179
Baiae, 153–4
Beaujolais, 79, 157
Beaune, 157
Beer, 124
Black Sea, 21, 76, 129, 133
Boeotia, 103, 114
Bolshevist Revolution, 40
Bordeaux, 157
Boreas, 39
Bosphorus, 129
Bourgeois god, 25
Brandy, 143, 155
Briseis, 36
Britain, 97, 158
   *see also* England
Bromios, 55–7, 62, 101–2, 106–7,
   156, 163, 182
Brygos painter, 11
Buddhists, 65
Bull(s), 51, 58–60
Bull god, 51
Bull's head, 52–3, 83
Bull's horns, 56
Burgundy, 139, 143, 155, 157
Byron, 72
Byzantine(s), 62, 71–2

Cadiz, 72
Cadmus, 55–6, 60–1
Caecubum, Caecuban, 153
Caere, Caeretan, 83
Caesar, 166
Calabria, 148
Cales, Calenum, 154
Caligula, 154
   *see also* Gaius

Campania, 153–4, 159
Cana of Galilee, 79
Canaan, Canaanite, 17 f., 21, 150
Candia, 73–6
Canea, 76
Capri, 130
Caria, 21
Cassandra, 166
Castalia, 67
Cathars, 40
Catherine of Siena, St, 64
Cato, 140, 152
Caucasus, 15, 16, 24
Cephalonia, 75
Cephissus, 114
Ceres, 156
Chablis, 157
Chalcedon, 133
Chalcidian, 83
Chalybon, 20
Champagne, 143, 155, 157
"Château Neuf du Cardinal", 158
Cher, 157
Chianti, 141
China, 21
Chios, Chian, 73–4, 77, 83, 92, 119,
    132, 141
Chous, 136–7
Christ, 62–3
    see also Jesus
Christendom, 126–7, 171–3, 175
Christian(s), Christianity, 40, 123,
    151–2, 171, 174–5
Christos Pantocrator, 62
Chryseis, 35–6
Chrysostom, 175
Church, the, 40, 62, 122
    Eastern, 175, 177
    Militant, 65
Cider, 92
Cilicia, Cilician, 20, 24, 25
Cincius, 122
Circe, 43
Cithaeron, 55–6, 58, 60, 103
Clarence, Duke of, 72
Claret, 143, 157
Claudius, 123, 171

Clazomenae, 83
Cleisthenes, 102
Clement of Alexandria, 174–5
Cleopatra, 123
Clytaemnestra, 96
Cnidos, Cnidian, 134–5
Cnossos, see Knossos
Coffee, 68
Cognac, 143
Coitus, 94
Columella, 140, 153
Comedy, 104
Commendaria, 76
Constantine, 171
Constantinople, 73, 123–4
Corcyra, Corcyraean, 41, 132, 135
Corfu, 76, 130
Corinth, Corinthian, 67, 76, 83, 102,
    132, 135, 165–6, 180
Corinthus (plate dealer), 165
Corn, 131
Corsica, 129
Corycian Cave, 107–8, 179
Côte d'Azur, 136
Côte-Rôtie, 157
Crete, Cretan, 27, 51–3, 72, 130, 133
Crimea, 82, 133
Crisa, 102
Cumae, 159–60, 165, 167
Cybele, 56
Cyclops, Cyclopes, 35, 46–8, 165
Cypris, 121–2, 124
    see also Kypris
Cyprus, Cyprian, 27, 51, 53, 57,
    72–7, 83, 120, 130
Cythera, 120


Daedalus, 34, 166
Damas, 164
Damascus, 20
Danaans, 42
Daphni, 173–4
Dardanelles, 27
Datames, 23, 25
Dead Sea, 18
defrutum, 152

Delos, 83
Delphi, Delphian, 66–7, 101, 102, 104–9, 114, 179
Demeter, 22, 25, 50, 113, 124, 131, 156, 182
    Thesmophoros, 97
Demo, 122, 125
Demosthenes, 39, 137
Despotiko, 130
Diagon, 137
Diana, 168
Diocletian, 151
Diomede, 116, 167
Dionysia, 100, 103
Dionysius, St, 176
Dionysos, Dionysiac, 1, 9–10, 13, 23, 25–7, 31, 40, 49–66, 68, 78, 93–4, 98, 100–8, 131, 133, 144, 149–51, 155–7, 164, 172–3, 176–9, 182
    see also Bacchos, Bromios
Dnieper, 135
Dodona, Dodonean, 38
Dog-Star, 127
dolia, 152
Donoussa, 130
Doris, 124–5
Dorkis, 120
Dorset, 158
Duronia, 145

Echion, 61
Egypt, Egyptian, 17, 52–3, 62, 86, 112
Eleusis, 105, 113, 173
Eleutherae, 103, 105
Elis, 48
Encolpius, 159, 171
England, 72, 158
    see also Britain
Ennakrounos, 67
enthousiasmos, 53
Enyalios, 50
Epernay, 157
Ephesians, Epistle to, 20
Epigrams, 117

Epiktetos, 11
Erasmus, 72
Ergotimos, 87
Eros, 120, 172–3
Erymanthus, 137
Erythrae, 27
Eshcol, 18
Ethiopia, Ethiopians, 16, 161
Etna, 133, 138
Etruria, Etruscans, Tuscan, 82–3, 141–2, 144–5, 152, 156
Euanthes, 46
Euboea, 132–3
Euenos, 117–18
Euhios, 55, 57
Euohi, Evoe, 55, 57, 107
Euneus, 44
Euripides, 54–5, 61–2, 65, 97, 100, 102, 107, 108, 149, 182
    see also Bacchae; Ion
Europa, 51
Europe, 62
Eve, 18, 125
Exekias, 88

Falernum, Falerna, Falernian, 153–154, 158, 167
Fates, 56
Fathers of the Church, 171, 174–5
Faustianum, 153
Fecenia, Hispala, 146–7
"Festival Women", 97
Feuer, L. S., 126–7
Fire Brigade, 171
Flamininus, 149
Flood, the, 16–17
Floor-show, 2, 167
Florence, 87
Fortunata, 160, 162, 164, 166, 170–171
Forum Appii, 153
Foundry painter, 11
France, French, 40, 71, 78, 97, 142–3, 156–7
Francis (of Assisi), St, 63
French Revolution, 40

Freud, S., 66, 126
Fufluns, 144, 156
Fundi, Fundanum, Fundanian, 153–154

Gadara, Gadarene, 119
Gaius, 171
  see also Caligula
Galatea, 125
Galen, 154
Gales painter, 11
Gallo-Germanic, 157
Ganymede, 35, 167–8
Ganymede (character in *Satyricon*), 160
Gaul, 65, 130, 142, 156
Gauranum, 154
Genesis, 16, 17
Geoponic collection, 140
George, St, 176
Georgian, 15
Gephyraioi, 114
Germany, German, Germanic, 71, 82
Germanos, Archbishop, 73
Gibbon, Edward, 150
Gibraltar, 129
Gilgamesh, 17
Giton, 159, 168, 171
Glass, 166
Glauke, 67
*gleukos*, 70, 152
Goat-singers, 103
Gorgo, 96
Granicus, 27
Grape-vine, wild, 15
Graves, 157
Gregory, Patriarch, 73
Griffins, 51
*Guide Bleu* (Greece), 68
Guyon, Madame, 63

Habinnas, 160, 169–71
Hades, 38, 121, 124
Hadrian, 122–3, 171
Hagia Sophia, 123

Ham, 16, 17
Hamath, 18
Hampshire, 158
Hampton Court, 158
Hannibal, 165
Harmodios, 114–16
Hebe, 35
Hebrew, 16–17, 119, 150
Hector, 32, 37, 39
Hecuba, 37
Hekamede, 43
Helen, 36–7, 168
Helicon, 67
Heliodoros, 121
Helios, 133
Hellenistic, 27
Hellespont, Hellespontine, 27, 31, 129
Helli, 38
Henderson, A., *History of Ancient and Modern Wines*, 72
Hephaistos (Hephaestus), 33, 35, 117
*hepsema*, 70, 152
Hera, 22, 35, 49
Heraklea, 130
Herakles, 93
Hermeros, 166
Hermes, 50
Hermione, 118
Hermitage, 75, 157
Hesiod, 27, 121
Hestia, 66
*Hetaira(i)*, 94, 95, 112
Hieron, 67
Hindus, 65
Hipparchos, 114–16
Hippias, 114–15
Hippocrene, 67
Hitler, A., 40
Hittite(s), 15, 24–5, 50
Hock, 140, 143
Homer, Homeric, 8, 27, 32–48, 49–50, 83, 93, 102, 116, 121, 130, 157, 165, 167–8, 173, 181
  see also *Iliad*, *Odyssey*
Homosexuality, 122, 126
Horace, 154

Hosea, 19
Hyampia, 106
Hygieia, 35
Hymettus, 79
Hypsipyle, 44

Icaria, 132
Ida, 76
Idaeus, 37
Idomeneus, 42
*Iliad*, 32–49
Ilium, 165
   *see also* Troy
Imbros, 31
India, 21
Ion, 108
*Ion* (Euripides), 108
Ionia, Ionian, 27, 44, 95, 101, 141–142
Ionian Sea, 130
Iphigenia, 168
Iran, 21
   *see also* Persia
Iris, 35, 39
Isaiah, 19
Ischia, 130
Ismarus, 46
Israel, Israelites, 17, 18, 148
Italy, Italian, 133, 140, 142, 147–8, 152–3, 156–7, 159–60, 171
Itea, 106
Ithaca, 75
Ivriz, 22, 24, 25, 28

Japheth, 17
Jason, 44
Jehonadab, 150
Jehu, 150
Jeremiah, 150
Jerez, 72
Jericho, 19
Jerusalem, 19
Jesus, 41, 63, 64, 79
   *see also* Christ
Jews, 16, 79

John Chrysostom, St, 175
John the Evangelist, St, 79
Julius Proculus, Caius, 163
Jupiter, 164, 166
Justinian, 123, 125

Kallias, 2–5, 7, 10, 110
Kalliroe, 67
Kallistion, 120
Kallisto, 11
Katherina, 6
Kent, 158
King-priest, 24, 28
Klea, 105
Kleitias, 87
Klepsydra, 67
Knights of Malta, 76
Knossos, 34, 51, 53
Komodoi, 104
*komos*, 93
*kottabos*, 110–12
Kotyle, 136–7
Kouphos, 130
Kritobulos, 5
Kronos, 56
Kurds, 20
Kyathos, 136–7
Kypris, 118
   *see also* Cypris
Kythera, 129

Lacrima Christi, 157
*lagoenae*, 152
Lampsakos, Lampsacene, 27–9, 31
Languedocs, 40
Lares, 168
Latin(s), Latium, 142, 144, 153–4, 156, 167
Lawson, J. C., 178
Lebadeia, 105
Lemnos, 44
Leodes, 42
Lesbos, 44, 74, 92, 112, 117, 132
Les Fontaines, 64
Libation, 35, 36, 38, 41

# INDEX

Liber, 156, 164
Libera, 156
Libya, 82
Liebfraumilch, 157
Livy, 144, 148, 151
Loire, 157
Lot, 18, 19
Loukoumi, 80
Love, 118, 171
Loves, the, 121, 126
Luke, Gospel of, 19
Lusitania, 137
Luwian, 15
Lycia, 21
Lyde, 120-1
Lydia, Lydian, 21, 56, 122, 141
Lykaon, 2, 10
Lykourgos, 49
Lysistrata (Aristophanes), 96, 97,
    105

Macedon, Macedonia, 54, 61, 78, 133,
    136-7, 177
Machaon, 43
Mâcon, 157
Madeira, 72, 75, 78
Maenads, 26, 56-7, 65, 93, 103-4,
    177, 179
Mahomet, see Mohammad
Malaga, 78
Malmsey, 71-2, 74, 76, 78
Malta, 129
Malvoisie, 71
Mani, 125
Marathon, 79, 113
Marcius Philippus, Q., 144
Marcus Argentarius, 122
Marcus Aurelius, 171
Margaret Marie Alacoque, St, 64
Markopoulo, 79
Marlay painter, 12
Maro, 46
Maronea, 68
Mars, 158
Marsala, 72
Marseilles, 130, 142-3

Marsyas, 162
Martial, 141
Martyrologists, 151
Mary, the Virgin, 78-9
Massalia, see Marseilles
Massicum, 154
Mazaeus, 25
Media, Medes, 20, 106, 113
Mediterranean, 129, 131, 136
Médoc, 157
Memory, 121
Mende, Mendaean, 68, 91, 132,
    137
Menelaus, 36-7, 42-4
Mentes, 41
Mesopotamia, 17, 20, 21, 149
Messalina, 123
Messene, 96
Mesta, 77
Meursault, 157
Mexico, Mexican, 40
Middle Ages, 54, 95
Mika, 98-100
Miletus, 27, 120
Mimnermus, 120-1
Mingrelian, 15
Minoan(s), 17, 45, 52-3
Minos, 49, 51
Missolonghi, 72
Mithridates, 167
Mnesilochus, 98-100
Moab, Moabites, 19
Mohammad, 150-1
Monastic, Monasticism, 172
Monemvasia, 71
Montmartre, 158
Montrachet, 157
Mormons, 151
Moselle, 143, 157
Moses, 18
Moslems, 65, 151, 172
Mother of God, 78
    see also Mary, Virgin
Mummius, 166
Muses, 35, 57, 121
mustum, 152
Musulmans, see Moslems

Mycenae, Mycenaean, 15, 17, 28, 32, 45, 50
  tablets, 50, 102
Myrmidons, 38
Myron (sculptor), 101
Myrtle-branch, 111–12, 114, 116
Mysia, North, 27
Mystery, 106
Mysticism, Mystic, Mystical, 54, 59, 62, 65–6, 107
Mytilene, 119

Nanno, 120–1
Naples, Neapolitan, 119, 130, 152, 154, 157
"Napoleon" brandy, 143
Nasta, 167
"National Anthem", Athenian, 116
Navel-stone, 102
Naxos, 74, 132, 138, 176
  (Sicily), 133
Nectar, Nektar, 35, 48, 77
Nereids, 178–9
Nero, 123, 142, 159, 153, 159, 171
Nestor, 43
  cup of, 43, 45, 83
New York, 152
Nice (Nicea), 130, 143
Nikagoras, 119
Nike, 35
Nikeratos, 5, 8
Nile, 123
Niobe, 166
Noah, 16, 17
Nuits, 157
Nymphs, 26, 118, 173, 177, 179

Ocean, 129
Odysseus, 35, 37, 41–3, 46–7, 50
  see also Ulysses
Odyssey, 32–48 passim
Oedipus, 66
Oenops, 42
Oil, 131
oinops, 48

oinos retinites, see retinites
Olbia, 135
Olive, 129, 133
Olympia, 67, 137
Olympias, 96
Olympus, Olympian, 27, 33, 35, 48, 53, 57, 61, 66, 113, 137
Olynthus, Olynthian, 52
Opimius, 158
Oporto, 137
Orion, 117
Orthodox Christians, 65
Orvieto, 141
Oscan, 144
Osiris, 62
Ostia, 153
Ouzo, 68, 137

Pachys, St, 176
Pacific, 94
Paestum, 130
Paion, 50
Palestine, 17–18, 41, 119
Palm-trees, 129
Pan, 26, 113, 173, 177, 179, 180
Panathenaic Festival, Games, 2, 103, 109, 114
Pandemos, 120
Panopeus, 105
Papas, 78, 80
Pappus, St, 152
Parentium, 168
Parion, 27, 31
Paris, 36–7, 158
Parnassus, 106, 179
Parnes, 91
Paros, 27, 91, 176
Parthenon, 66, 83
Pasitheoi, 50
Patras, 73
Patroclus, 32, 37–40
Paul, St, 20, 125
Paul the Silentiary, 123–6
Pausanias, 105
Peasant god, 22, 24–5
Pegasus, 67, 162

Peirene, 67
Peisander, 6
Peisistratus, 62, 103, 105, 112, 114, 132, 149
Pelasgian Zeus, 38
Peloponnesus, 62, 71, 180
Pentelicus, 79
Pentheus, 55–61, 102, 149
Peparethos, 132
Pergamum, 117
Periander, 102
Pericles, 39
Perkote, 27, 31
Persephone, 113, 123–4
Persia, Persian, 20, 25, 72, 99
    see also Iran
Petraites, 166
Petronius, 158–60, 171
Petruchio, 6
Phaleron, 10
Pharnabazus, 25
Philip, 4, 6, 7
Philippides, 113
Philippos, 11
Philistia, 82
Philodemus, 119, 122
Phintias, 112
Phocaea, 27
Phoenicia, 121
Phrygia(n), 21, 44, 54, 56
    Minor, 27
Picasso, P., 88
Pieria, 57
Pindar, 67–8
Pine cones, 70–1
Pines, 129
Piraeus, 2, 10
pithoi, 70–1, 152
Pittalokos, 126
Plataea, 105
Plato, Platonic, 1, 2, 8, 9, 39, 91
    see also Symposium
Pleistos, 106
Pliny, 101, 140, 153–4
Ploutos, 113
Plutarch, 105
Police, Chief of, 150

Polygnotos, 12
Polynesia, 94
Pomerol, 157
Pompeii, 135, 167
Pompeius Diogenes, Caius, 163
Pomptine Marshes, 153
Pontic, 83
Pontonous, 41
Poppaea, 123
Port, 35, 44, 71–2, 139
Porter, in Macbeth, 118
Poseidippos, 120
Poseidon, 50–1
Postumius Albinus, Sp., 144, 147
Pouilly Fuissé, 157
Pramnian (wine), 43–4
Priam, 44
Priansos, 27
Priapos, Priapus, 26–31, 168
Pronomos painter, 13
Proserpina, 156
Protestants, 65, 172
Provence, 126, 143, 157
Proverbs, Book of, 19
Psycho-analysis, 126–7
Puteoli, 154
Pyrgos, 48
Pythagoras, 117
Pythia, 102
Pythian Games, 102

Quakers, 66
Queens' College, Cambridge, 72

Rain-maker, 177
Rechab, Rechabites, 19, 150
Rehob, 18
    relationships, 26
Resin, 77
resinatum, 152
Rethymo, 76
retinites, 71, 91, 152
retsina, resinated, 68, 71, 77–8, 91, 138
Rheims, 157

Rhine, Rhineland, 71, 142, 157
Rhodes, Rhodian, 83, 92, 130, 132–134
Rhodope, 124
Rhone, 76, 142–3, 157
Riesling, 157
Riviera, Italian, 136
Roman Catholics, 65
Roman Empire, 62
Rome, Roman(s), 27, 71, 119, 132, 137, 139, 141–2, 144–5, 147–52, 156–9, 171, 181–2
Rosé d'Anjou, 157
Russia, 40, 76

Sabaean, 16
Sabazios, 50
Sabine, 144
Saint-Emilion, 157
St Lawrence river, 129
Salt Lake City, 151
Samaritan, Good, 19
Samos, Samian, 72, 118, 119–20, 133
Santorini, 74, 76, 91
Sanudo, Marco, 177
Saône, 143
Sardinia, 130
Sardis, 122
Satyricon (Petronius), 158–9
Satyrs, 26, 173, 177, 179, 180
Saumur, 157
Sauternes, 157
Scintilla, 160, 170
Scio, 74, 77
Scipio, 149
Scissa, 169
Scythian policeman, 100
Seals, 133
Seilenos, Silenus, 26, 93, 103, 173, 176
Seilens, 26
Seleucus, 121
Semele, 49, 50, 55, 57
Semitic, 15
Sempronius Rutilus, T., 145
Senate, Senators, Roman, 147–9

Setia, Setinum, Setinian, 153
Shem, 16, 17
Sherry, 71–2, 155
Shiraz, 72
Sibyl, 165
Sicily, 72, 96, 130, 133, 135, 165
Sicyon, 102
Sidon, 121
Silenus, see Seilenos
Sinuessa, 153
Sirius, 127
Skiathos, 136
Skinoussa, 130
Skolion, skolia, 110–28
Smyrna, 44, 75, 101
Socrates, 1–13 passim, 14, 91, 110
Sodom and Gomorrah, 18
Soloi, 27
Solomon, 151
Sophocles, 54
Sorrento, 130, 154
Spain, Spanish, 78, 149, 169
Sparta, Spartiate(s), 95, 96, 113, 117, 132
Statinian, 153
Stavros, 79
Strabo, 153
Strato, 122–3
Sudan, 82
Sulla, 153
Sunium, 27, 31, 79
Surrentinum, 154
Sussex, 158
Switzerland, 97
Sylvaner, 157
Symposium
  Plato's, 1–3, 9, 13, 91
  Xenophon's, 1–2, 20, 110, 161
Syracuse, Syracusan, 4–6, 8–9, 132, 141
Syria, Syrian, 17, 119–21
Syrus, 166

Tacitus, 159
Tanagra, 114
Tarentum, 66, 94, 165

Tarsus, 20, 23–5, 125
Tauromenium, 138
Taurus, 24–5
Tavel, 157
Tebessa, 136
Telemachus, 41–2
Tenedos, 43, 74–5
Tenos, 75
Terpander, 112
Terracina, 165
Thasos, Thasian, 132, 134
Theatre, 104, 106
Thebes, Theban, 55–6, 59, 61, 105
Theocritus, 118
Theopompus, 141–2
Thera, 74, 138
Theresa (of Avila), St, 63
Thermion, 122
Theseus, 93
*Thesmophoriazusae*, 97
Thesmophorion, 97–8
Thespis, 104
Thessaly, 44, 133
Thetis, 32, 49
*thiasos*, 93
Thirty Years War, 40
Thrace, Thracian, 15, 50, 54, 68, 102, 124, 127–8, 177
Thyiads, 26, 101, 104–9, 177
Tiber, 144
Tiberius, 154, 156
Tigellinus, 159
Tigris, 20
Timaeus, of Syracuse, 141
Timaeus, of Tauromenium, 92
Tiresias, 55–6, 61
Titus, 171
Tmolus, 55
Tokay, 76
    Imperial, 20
Tragedy, 104
Tragodoi, 103, 104
Trajan, 171
Traminer, 157
Trapezus, Trapezuntines, 20–1, 133
Trebizond, *see* Trapezus
Trimalchio, 156–72 passim

Tripod, 102
"Trireme, the", 92
Tritons, 92
Trojan horse, 166
Troubadours, 126
Troy, Trojan, 32, 35–9, 42–4, 47, 96, 168
    *see also* Ilium
Turkestan, 15
Turks, Turkish, 73, 80
Turkish delight, 68
Tuscan(s), Tuscany, *see* Etruria
Tyana, 24
Tydeus, 116
Tyrants, 55


Ulysses, 165
    *see also* Odysseus
Urbana Colonia, 153
Ursula, St, 152
Usher, Archbishop, 17
Utah, 151


Vappa, woppa, wop, 152, 154
Varro, 140, 152, 153
Vases, shapes of, ch. VI passim
Vatican hill, 41
Venice, Venetian, 73
Vespasian, 171
Vesuvius, 138
Victoria, 171
Vines, dwarf and climbing, 68
    *see also* Grape-vine
Virgil, 153
*Vitis vinifera*, 14 n.
Vlachs, 177
Vouliagmeni, 129
Vouvray, 157


Water, 67–8
    mixing with wine, 91
Whisky, Scotch, 92
Wight, Isle of, 158
Winds, 39

Wine, colours of, 138–40
Wine-coins, 133, 140
Wine-merchant, 32
Wolsey, 158
Wop, *see* Vappa
Wreck, 136

Xanthippe, 6
Xenophon, 1–2, 9–10, 12–14, 20, 82, 110, 161
   *Anabasis*, 20
   *Symposium*, *see* Symposium

Xuthos, 108

Zacha, 138
Zacynthus, 48
Zante, 74, 76
Zephyr, 39
Zeus, 25, 35, 37–8, 41, 47, 49–51, 56–7, 112–13, 177
   from Artemisium, 83
Zim, 18
Zoar, 19